Senegal Parrot

Senegal Parrots as pets.

Senegal Parrots Essential Owners Guide

By

Charles Wells

Table of Contents

Introduction

Senegal parrots, or Poicephalus Senegalus, belong to the Poicephalus family, and they are the most popular parrots out of this genus. These parrots are well known for their exceptional pet quality, stillness, and extraordinary calm temperament. Senegal parrots inhabit open woodlands and savannas of western Africa, from Guinea and Cameroon to Chad. Senegal parrot's color mutations are the pied colored and very rare yellow colored birds. In the wild, these naturally shy birds build their nests in holes of trees, and they usually live in pairs or small flocks.

Senegal parrots' plumage presents mostly shades of green, the feathers on the head are brownish- parrot color, the "V" shaped patch on their abdomen ranges from yellow to orange. The beak and feet are parrot color, and the eyes are light yellow. Their mainly green plumage provides perfect camouflage when roosting in trees.

Senegal parrots have a comparatively large head and beak for their overall size. They are relatively small birds in comparison with other parrot species, growing to 9.05 inches (23cm) in length.

The youngsters have dark parrot-black irises, but with maturity, they will become yellow. In adulthood, the parrot color is a bit darker than on youngsters.

Senegal parrots' relatively small size and charming personality make them the perfect parrot for many people. They make a good companion and are considerably friendly compared to other parrot species.

Chapter 1: Pet Parrots

Some people enjoy bird ownership because they require only a minimal amount of grooming. Birds, in fact, seem to take a certain amount of pride in keeping themselves clean. They preen their feathers every day, keeping them shiny and clean. The most help they need from you is a quick trim of their nails now and then.

Another reason why parrots make such popular pets is their ability to socialize with their owners. To those individuals who know little about parrots, it may not seem like a parrot would be a pet that would bond with his owner. But, indeed, he is.

You'd be surprised that many parrot owners take their birds with them when they run their daily errands, taking their feathered friends to the bank or grocery store.

Parrots are entertaining. It's a fact. In many ways, parrots are the clowns of the bird world. They possess a wide range of comical behavior patterns that can keep you entertained for hours. Ask any individual who owns a parrot, and he'll tell you that the mere presence of a parrot in his home seems to bring a natural vibrancy and life to the home.

While the longevity of a bird may be a disadvantage to many, to parrot lovers it's a great benefit. You're unlikely to deal with very many grieving experiences when you adopt a parrot. It may very well be the only parrot you ever own, for as long as the bird's lifespan.

To Speak or Not to Speak: Will My Bird Talk?

A unique attraction of parrots is their ability to speak. Many potential parrot owners choose to have a pet parrot, especially for this reason. So how can you be sure that the bird you're considering adopting will eventually talk? The truth is you'll never know for sure; talking is merely a matter of probability – not certainty. Certain choices can increase the odds of having a bird that talks.

But more than that, he's more likely to keep learning throughout his entire life.

You can also choose certain species of parrots who are known to be easier to train and are known as "talkers." One of these is the Senegal Parrot. This bird is also known for his ability to adopt a large vocabulary and for his native intelligence.

In addition to that, he's a stunningly beautiful bird, with brilliantly colored feathers.

Don't Think Parrots Are Low Maintenance

Frustrating. Time-consuming. Even exhausting. These are all words used by those individuals who keep parrots as pets. It's no secret that these birds demand more time and effort than many people would like to think – or expect.

In some cases, people adopt parrots not knowing how complex a creature they are. Being highly intelligent, this animal demands more of your time than your average dog or cat.

You can expect a complex creature that has various needs and quite a few desires. If these needs and desires aren't met, not only can these birds come down with physical illnesses, they may also develop psychological problems as well. They don't do well being alone. And if they don't have other birds to interact with, they'll adopt you as another bird.

They make noises at these particular hours because these are innate calling and gathering times for them. If you walk out of the room, the odds are very good that they'll call to get you back in there with them.

Parrots Are Not Neat

It's a parrot fact of life: Parrots are messy. Their cages require frequent cleaning (and by the way, birds can defecate every 10 or 15 minutes), and they are extremely messy eaters. Before you decide to adopt one, take a look at the pet store at feeding time. It could make even the most ardent parrot lover think twice about adopting one!

Okay, here's another disadvantage to parrot ownership. They bite - even the tamest of pet parrots will occasionally bite. Why? A variety of reasons – and sometimes it's not easy trying to figure out exactly why! Sometimes, they'll bite out of fear, or they just may be doing it out of boredom. Parrots also bite out of frustration or for reasons related to their innate territorial instincts. Indeed, parrots are truly complex animals.

Character

Senegal parrots' relatively small size and charming personality make them the perfect parrot for many people. They make a good companion and are considerably friendly related to other parrot species.

The Senegal parrot is considered to be quieter than most parrot species, but they are still capable of loud screams and vocalizations. They have exceptional pet quality, extraordinarily calm temperament and are well known for their quietness. Their talking voices are gentle and delicate.

Senegal parrots are not good at imitating human speech in comparison with other parrots species (like African Grey Parrots), but they are still able to learn up to 15-20 words or phrases. These birds can also imitate sounds of phones and other electrical appliances, the sounds of other animals, human voices, and whistles. Senegal parrots are extremely intelligent birds; they can learn tricks, they love human interaction, but are also able to entertain themselves while the owner is gone. Senegal parrots are cuddly and devoted, playful and loving, but they need to socialize well with other people because they may develop phobias and can become one-person birds. They can become jealous of other family members or pets and may attack larger birds or dogs if they feel that their owner is threatened.

Senegal parrots that are properly cared for generally have sweet, charming personalities and they can make tame pets. Senegal parrots love playing, climbing and are often seen hanging upside down. To keep them happy, all you need to do is to make sure that there are toys (plastic chains, perches, swings, ladders), pieces of wood (from which they can nibble) and tree branches available for them. They manifest wild behavioral characteristics, which we usually can't see in dogs or cats, that`s why they are considered wild animals.

In the wild, if a member of a flock learns a new skill, then the other members will copy that new skill because it plays an important role in their survival. Wild parrots have to be ready to protect their territory, to find food and water, to avoid raptors, to defend their pair and to transmit these qualities to their descendants.

So if you decide to bring a parrot as a pet in your house, you'll have to know that you will need to dedicate time, patience and affection, every single day to your bird.

Your bird will need to learn to cooperate, to tolerate environmental changes and to accept veterinary care and examinations. S/he has to develop a strong sense of its personality, otherwise, if a bird doesn't learn to clean itself or to play when s/he is alone, after all, s/he will decide that the owner can satisfy every kind of their necessity. You'll have to guide your bird towards an acceptable behavior because it's much easier to prevent bad behaviors, rather than change them.

Because in the wild, parrots used to live in holes of trees, it`s very important to offer them wood sticks to chew.

Parrots usually represent a very long-term responsibility, and they are not the perfect choice for everyone. Chasing a sensitive and frightened bird and trying to catch it and comfort it is the last thing we want to do. This is the perfect example of how our bird will lose confidence in us. In these situations, the best thing is to leave the bird alone until it has calmed down.

A Senegal parrot that is neglected could be destructive and noisy, and they are behaving naughty because they want attention. If s/he starts screaming for attention and you scream back at the bird, then what you have done is reinforced the bad behavior of the bird.

Screaming out of boredom is another common situation among Senegals. To stop excessive screaming, first you need to change your interaction with your bird, then try to get a bigger cage, add more natural branches and wood to chew on, replace the old toys with new ones as frequently as possible. If by mistake, you taught your bird that it would get your attention when it screams, then you must stop giving it any attention and give it attention when it is quiet and behaves nicely.

Some people think that their bird will bite them. The bird won't bite you as long as you try to manipulate the bird by using your hands and fingers in a friendly and calm way. People used to react when the bird wants to step up on their finger by grabbing the finger with its beak, and people think that the bird it`s going to bite, and they pull their finger away.

But all s/he wants is to step up on your finger, because s/he thinks it`s a branch of a tree. If you pull your finger away, it`s going to grab and hold your finger with her/his beak, and you will reinforce the bird for another bad habit, and s/he will realize, that if s/he grabs your finger, it will cause another reaction, another drama. So you have to use positive reinforcement for behavior not resulting in biting. Don't forget, they do have the potential to become very cuddly and devoted birds, and they tend to become attached to their owners.

Youngsters should be socialized to many people and exposed to a variety of situations such as handling by friends, visits to the veterinarian, nail and wing clips, to avoid the fear of new situations. Young Senegal parrots that grow up near other Senegal parrots are less likely to be emotionally unstable because they are capable of studying and learning the more experienced bird's behavior.

Getting to know someone that has experience raising Senegal parrots will help you decide if they are the right birds for you.

Parrots can also produce a powder-like substance, which helps them to clean and to protect their feathers, but it may cause allergies to humans.

Respiratory organs

Birds have a single nasal cavity, and the larynx does not have vocal cords, it helps only to lock trachea during swallowing. They have lungs, and they also have nine air sacs through which air circulates. These air sacs allow a continuous flow of air through the respiratory system.

Digestive components

The beak serves to pick up food and for seed peeling.

The crop is the muscular pouch, and it can be found at the end of the esophagus and serves as a chamber for storing and softening food until the food already in the stomach moves on through the rest of the digestive system.

The crop leads to a two-chambered stomach: one called proventriculus, which has the role to produce stomach enzymes for breaking food down, and the other chamber called ventriculus or gizzard, a powerful muscular organ, which takes the place of teeth and here the seeds and an assortment of grains of sand are squeezed until the seeds break up into a digestible form.

From here, the food goes through the thin then thick intestine and the digested food arrives in the cloaca. The cloaca is the final part of a digestive tract, and it is a small chamber with a mucous membrane. Parrots excrete their feces and their urine from the cloaca, and it also plays an important role in reproduction.

Urinary tract organs

The kidneys of the birds are located on both sides of the backbone, and the air sacs protect them. The urine will be eliminated through the cloaca, and it can be a soft or solid substance, and it contains uric acid which makes it very corrosive.

Genital organs

Cocks have testicles and females have ovaries inside the body, and when the birds are ready to breed, their reproductive organs (testes and ova) swell and produce the sperm and ova. For cocks, the sperm is stored in the cloaca, until an opportunity to mate arises, and hens will receive the sperm into their cloaca before it fertilizes their ova.

Females have only one ovary and one oviduct, but in early stages of embryonic development each female bird has two ovaries, and only the left ovary develops into a functional organ. During the breeding season, the size of the ovary is changing, becoming larger. Males have paired abdominal testes which can be found inside of the cavity of the body. During breeding season the testes increase in size, becoming almost five times bigger than the initial size.

Body temperature is between 104 - 105.8 degrees Fahrenheit (40-41 degrees Celsius), which increase by 32.9 degrees Fahrenheit (0.5 degrees Celsius) during sexual maturity, during the egg-laying process and in molting period.

The eyes

Most of the birds have their eyes placed on each side of the head. With the help of their mobile neck, bird`s can see the surroundings in a radius of 360 degrees and can fly away rapidly if there is any danger nearby. The lower eyelid of the bird is mobile, and the upper one is almost fixed. The third eyelid, which is called nictitating membrane, is hinged at the inner side of the eye, and it serves to protect the eyes from bright light, wind, etc....

The Ears

The ears are tiny, round holes situated on the right and left the side of the head, behind the eyes and they are covered with feathers. There are no cartilaginous pavilions, but inside the ear, there is the organ of balance. When the bird suffers from ear diseases, the organ of balance is also affected. The sick bird can`t hold itself properly on the perches, and its head is twisting to the affected ear.

Lifespan

In captivity, birds can live much longer than in the wild, with the condition that they get all the necessary nutrition and care which they need. Even in captivity, the lack of food, incomplete diet and improper care of parrots could lead to a considerably shorter lifespan. Senegal parrot's average lifespan is 15-20 years in the wild and over 30 years in captivity.

Senegal parrots are very lovely exotic birds, so if you want to be happy with your bird, you have to study your parrot's personality and abilities, which will help to create a perfect pet-owner relationship, leading to a happy life together.

If you ask a few people who wish to have an exotic bird about what they are expecting from the bird, the answer will be: to be smart, to be beautiful, to be able to learn to speak as fast as possible, to have a perfect singing voice, to be a clean bird, without damaging things in the house and the cost for everyday needs of the bird to be as cheap as possible. Before you decide to purchase a bird, you have to be aware of the fact that very few birds could match your expectations and you have to realize that these birds will be your companions for many years.

Don't forget that your bird will need food, cage cleaning and at least once a day fresh water. Your bird needs your companionship and affection, and it's very important to spend a few moments daily with it.

If you are uncertain about keeping a pair or just a single parrot, then you have to take into consideration that a single bird is much easier to maintain and to train. But if you don't have enough time to spend with him/her every single day, then I would strongly recommend buying a pair instead of a single bird.

If you decide to purchase a single bird, but you are uncertain about the bird's gender, then you have to take into consideration that the males are ideal pet birds and can be more easily domesticated than females. Males are not as noisy and destructive as females during the breeding period, and they can learn much easier to speak, because of their capacity for imitation.

Senegal parrots should not be allowed unsupervised freedom in the house because they can easily ingest harmful household toxins or dangerous items.

Another piece of advice: take the bird with you if you are going on holiday, because they just love going on holiday and love spend all their time with you and your family.

How to purchase a healthy bird

Purchasing a bird directly from the breeder or the pet store has multiple advantages. You can get information about their health condition, their provenience and also you can check the quality of the environment where they've been kept. You have to know a few aspects which could indicate hidden diseases: the bird has to be active with a good stability on its feet; the nostrils must be clean without secretion; the feathers around the beak must be clean; the birds breathe should be clear without whistling sounds; the eyes have to be clear; the missing feathers from the wings or tail could indicate "french molting"- viral disease which leads to feather loss; dirty feathers (with feces) at the tail area could indicate digestive system problems.

Life with cage birds

You need to prepare your house for the newly arrived parrot.

Before you bring your beloved bird in your house, first you have to find a proper place for it. It means that this place has to be quiet and without any air currents. The cage has to be equipped with all the necessary things: food, water, and toys. The first day it`s better to offer a little bit of privacy to the bird, even if we like to watch it, and it is recommended to cover the cage, especially during the day.

If you already own birds, the newly arrived bird has to be isolated in a separate cage (cages which are usually used for the transportation of the bird). You have to leave the bird to get used to the new conditions and with the new owner. Your parrot is considered accommodated when it does not get scared of the appearance of the owner, when s/he is feeding properly and when it's feathers look normal.

After the accommodation process, when you want to move your bird in another cage with the other birds, instead of stressing the bird by catching it with your hands, you better bring closer the entrances of the two cages and leave them in this position for a while, to give the chance to your bird to get into the other cage whenever s/he wants and when it is totally relaxed.

The transportation of parrots

Transportation of the birds can be dangerous when it's done improperly and can cause serious problems for your bird.

When you transport your bird from your vet or pet shop to your home it is recommended to keep it in a special cage (carrier) without water and food bowls, and toys in it, or in special carton boxes with tiny holes in them for the bird to be able to breathe and to avoid accidents. If you choose the cage, you better cover it with a piece of thin, dark-colored material and make sure that it has a hole on the top for the holder of the cage.

You can also transport your bird in a bigger shoebox with a lid. The box must have little holes in the sides so that the bird can breathe.

The parrot`s diet

When you purchase your bird, you have to know all about your bird's diet: what kind of food s/he has previously consumed. If the bird has not received the proper diet, then you have to replace it gradually. You'll need to offer your newly arrived bird freshwater and pieces of apples. If your bird presents signs of weakness, you'll have to offer some moist biscuits and egg paste; if s/he looks healthy, you can give your bird the usual food, but you can also add in his/her food some poppy seeds (it will have a calming effect on your bird). Chamomile tea (instead of water) also has a good calming effect and makes your bird feel more relaxed.

Chapter 2: To Buy or Not to Buy?

After learning what a Senegal parrot is, where they come from and how they live, this chapter will focus on giving you practical tips on what you need to know before buying one.

You will get a whole lot of information on its pros and cons, its average monthly costs as well as the things you need so that you will be well on your way to becoming a legitimate Senegal Parrot pet owner, should you decide to be one! It's up to you! Read on!

1. Pros and Cons of Senegal parrot

The information listed below is the advantages and disadvantages of owning a Senegal Parrot:

Pros

Personality: They are loving, playful and highly intelligent

Appearance: Has a beautifully crafted complexity

Noise: Parrots don't scream like other parrots, they only whistle, click and beep

Behavior: They can be single birds, unlike other bird species, parrots behaviors are highly individual.

Impact on Humans: You will find yourself constantly learning about these creatures. It will be an educational experience for you!

Cons

Personality: Quite sensitive, has a bit of a temper, needs lots of attention compared to other birds.

Cost: Price of the parrot ranges from $750 - $1,500 or more, it is quite expensive because it has better speaking skills than other bird species.

Damage to Your Home: They like to chew things. Do not leave them out of the cage unattended.

Behavior: They do not like to cuddle; they do not appreciate the intense physical contact. Just a few scratches will do!

Diet: They need more calcium than any other birds.

2.   Senegal Parrot Behavior with other pets

Some bird species are very welcoming to other pets but with parrots, not so much.

The Timneh may be more capable of accepting new family members than the Congo, but as with all birds, the behavior is highly individual. Nevertheless, parrots can learn to socialize and accept every member of the family. It depends largely on how you train it. Baby Senegal parrots often get along with other birds, but if a mature parrot is the first bird, it is more likely that it may not warm up to new birds unless they are carefully introduced.

Experts suggest that the best-behaved parrots are those who were exposed to lots of change in the environment, noises, and people because they become more adjusted.

3.   Ease and Cost of Care

Owning a Senegal Parrot is more expensive than an average bird, so make sure that before you buy one, you can cover the necessary costs it entails.

In this section, you will receive an overview of the expenses associated with purchasing and keeping a parrot as a pet. If you cannot cover these costs, a Senegal Parrot might not be the right pet for you.

Initial Costs

The initial expenses associated with keeping Senegal parrots as pets include the cost of the bird itself as well as the cage, cage accessories, toys, and grooming supplies.

You will find an overview of these costs below as well as the estimated total expense for keeping a Senegal Parrot:

Purchase Price: starts at $750 - $1,500

The price is higher for Senegal Parrots than the price for buying other types of parrots because of its ability to learn the nuances and intonation of human speech. Price also depends on the size of the bird.

Cage: starts at $250 - $500

You will need a large, strong and secure cage. Cages of this size do not come cheap! You should buy something that preferably has lots of space suitable for cage play and activity.

Accessories: more or less $100 in total

You will also need cage accessories like perches, lights, feeding dishes, stands, cage covers and harnesses for your Senegal Parrot. Accessories can be quite expensive depending on the brand as well as the quality of your purchase.

Toys: average total cost is $50

As one of the most clever parrot species, your Senegal Parrot needs plenty of stimulation to keep their intelligent and active minds entertained. Keep birdie boredom at bay with chewable toys for your Parrot.

Grooming Supplies: more, or less $70 in total

As part of pet hygiene, your feathered friend needs to be cleaned and properly groomed. There are lots of grooming supplies that you can buy online or at your local pet store.

Initial Cost for Senegal Parrot

Purchase Price $750 (£673)

Cage $250 (£224)

Accessories $100 (£89)

Toys $50 (£45)

Grooming Supplies $70 (£63)

Total $1,220 (£1095)

Monthly Costs

The monthly costs associated with keeping a Senegal Parrot are not for cheapskates! Some of the things that need to be bought on a monthly basis like food supplements, cleaning materials, and even veterinary care now and then will add up to your expenses. Below are the estimate monthly costs it entails.

Bird Food: approximately $30-$40 per month

Your Senegal Parrot needs a varied and healthy diet. There's a massive selection of high-quality seed diets, complete food and pelleted foods to choose from both online and in your local pet stores, as mentioned before, the cost will depend on the brand as well as the nutritional value of the food.

If your Senegal Parrot is a fussy feeder, then buy supplements with vitamins and minerals in, which you can add to either food or water.

Cleaning Supplies: at least $10 per month

You don't need brand new cleaning supplies every month, but of course, you will run out of bird shampoo and soap eventually. Just include it in your budget.

Veterinary Care: starts at $150 - $1,000 or more

Always take your parrot to an avian vet for any medical treatment. Avian vets are trained specifically to work with exotic birds, whereas a general practicing vet may not be familiar with their needs and treatments especially if they are sick, not to mention the medicines needed.

Additional Costs: at least $10 per month

In addition to all of these monthly costs, you should plan for occasional extra costs like repairs to your parrot cage, replacement toys, food supplements, medicines, etc. You won't have to cover these costs every month, but you should include it in your budget to be safe.

Monthly Costs for Senegal Parrot

Cost Type	Approximate Cost
Bird Food	$30 (£27)
Cleaning Supplies	$10 (£8)
Veterinary Care	$150 (£135)
Additional Costs	$10 (£8)
Total	$200 (£179)

4.   Tips in Buying a Senegal Parrot

If you are still interested in reading this chapter, that only means one thing: you have already decided to buy a Senegal Parrot!

Here you will learn tips and tricks on how to select a healthy parrot, where to find the right breeder, as well as the laws and permits you need to be aware of before buying.

1) Restrictions and Regulations in the United States

If you are planning to acquire a Senegal Parrot as your pet, then you have to think outside the cage. There are certain restrictions and regulations that you need to be aware of because it will not only serve as protection for your bird but also for you. Here are some things you need to know regarding the acquirement of Senegal Parrots, both in the United States and in Great Britain.

What is CITES?

CITES stands for Convention on International Trade in Endangered Species of Wild Fauna and Flora. It protects the wild Senegal Parrot by regulating its import, export, and re-export through an international convention authorized through a licensing system. It is also an international agreement, drafted by the International Union for Conservation of Nature (IUCN), which aims to ensure that the trade in specimens of wild animals and plants does not threaten their survival.

Different species are assigned in different appendix statuses such as Appendix I, II or III, etc. These appendices indicate the level of threat to the current population of the bird with consideration to their likely ability to rebound in the wild with legal trade. The Senegal Parrot is listed in Appendix I.

What is a CITES Permit?

CITES impose strict regulation on any species in Appendix I, which means that a permit is required to travel both to and from another country. A CITES permit is a document that confirms you have acquired your Senegal Parrot through authorized channels and have not indulged in the illegal pet trade that traps wild birds and exports them under horrific conditions in numbers that threaten their existence.

You must have a permit to leave your country; to enter another country; to leave that country and to re-enter your country otherwise it can lead to the confiscation of your bird.

The Division of Management Authority processes applications for CITES permits for the United States. You should allow at least 60 days for the review of your permit applications.

What is the purpose of CITES?

The Senegal Parrot is one of the targets of illegal trapping and is usually hunted for profit.

CITES purpose is to encourage support and commitment to a unified cause. However, it cannot enforce regulations in any nation and does not replace their existing law, that is why some countries continue to legally harvest Senegal Parrots with no consideration to their dwindling numbers, but since you are in U.S., you need to comply with the rules.

2) Permit in Great Britain and Australia

In Great Britain and Australia, you may need a permit for you to be able to import, export, or travel with your Senegal Parrot. This permit is called an Animal Movement License. It is required for the prevention of the spread of communicable diseases.

Like in the United States, getting a permit is a very important thing you need to consider before you acquire a bird because it is illegal to keep dangerous and endangered animals like a Senegal Parrot without legal permissions.

3) Practical Tips for Buying a Senegal Parrot

Now that you are already aware and have prior knowledge about the legal aspects of owning a Senegal Parrot, the next step is purchasing one through a local pet store or a legitimate breeder.

Here are some recommendations for finding a reputable Senegal Parrot breeder in the United States and United Kingdom.

a. How to Find a Senegal Parrot Breeder

The first thing you need to do is to look for a legit avian breeder or pet store in your area that specializes in Senegal Parrots.

You can also find great avian breeders online, but you have to take into consideration the validity of the breeder. It is highly recommended that you see your new bird in person before buying anything on the Internet. You can find several recommended lists of breeder websites later in this book.

Spend as much time as you can with your prospective new bird before you buy. Interact with the bird and see how it is with you.

Continue the diet of the bird as advised by the store owner or breeder to maintain its eating habits. Look for any health problems or issues as well.

Finally, only purchase a Senegal Parrot that is banded. Banding means the bird has a small metal band on one of its legs placed at birth by the breeder which is inscribed with the bird's clutch number, date of birth and the breeder number.

Leg bands are indicators that the purchaser and the bird itself are in the country legally and have not been smuggled.

b. Senegal Parrot Breeders in the United States

Here are the lists of Senegal Parrot breeders in the United States sorted by state.

If you don't find anyone near you, contact the closest one to your location and ask for a referral or a lead of the trusted breeders.

Parrots are very lovely exotic birds, so if you want to be happy with your bird, you have to study your parrot species' personality and abilities, which will help to create a perfect pet-owner relationship, leading to a happy life together.

If you ask a few people who wish to have an exotic bird about what they are expecting from the bird, the answer will be: to be smart, to be beautiful, to be able to learn to speak as fast as possible, to have a perfect singing voice, to be a clean bird, without damaging things in the house and the cost for everyday needs of the bird to be as cheap as possible. Before you decide to purchase a bird, you have to be aware of the fact that very few birds could match your expectations and you have to realize that these birds will be your companions for many years.

A parrot requires less time than a dog, and it`s easy to maintain, but don't forget that it will need food, cage cleaning and daily fresh water.

Your birds need your companionship and affection, and it`s very important to spend few moments daily with them.

If you are uncertain about keeping a pair or just a single parrot, then you have to take into consideration that a single bird is much easier to maintain and to train. But if you don't have enough time to spend with him/her every single day, then I would strongly recommend buying a pair instead of a single bird.

If you decide to purchase a single bird, but you are uncertain about the bird's gender, then you have to take into consideration that the males are ideal pet birds and can be more easily domesticated than females. Males are not as noisy and destructive as females during the breeding period, and they can learn much easier to speak, because of their capacity for imitation.

5. How to purchase a healthy bird

Purchasing a bird directly from the breeder or the pet store has multiple advantages. You can get information about their health condition, their provenience and also you can check the quality of the environment where they've been kept. You have to know a few aspects which could indicate hidden diseases: the bird has to be active with a good stability on its feet; the nostrils must be clean without secretion; the feathers around the beak must be clean; the birds breathe to be clear without whistling sounds; the eyes have to be clear; the missing feathers from the wings or tail could indicate "french molting"- viral disease which leads to feathers loss; dirty feathers (with feces) at the tail area could indicate digestive system problems.

Chapter 3: Life With Cage Birds

With some exceptions, parrots are sexually monomorphic, which means that their gender can't be determined by their markings or the color of their feathers. Differences in the appearance between the two genders are very small, and you can't recognize the gender of the bird by looking at it. The easiest and less expensive method for determining a parrot's gender is through quick DNA testing. There are lots of companies offering DNA testing as a mail-order service. You need some fresh cells of your bird so that DNA can be extracted from them. You can get some cells of your bird by carefully plucking 2-4 feathers off the chest of the bird.

This is a little bit painful for the bird but does not have any long-term effects. Feathers that are shed naturally are not suitable for extracting DNA (they lack blood and live cells). The pulled out feathers can be sent to a specialized laboratory that tells you the sex of birds.

You can also determine your parrot's gender after they've molted once. Males have a firm red tail on the underside of the secondary metrics, and those of the hen are tipped in grey color. Hens usually have a gradual dark to light grey color, from neck to belly, while males have a more uniform grey color in this area. The under tail coverts, which are located under the tail feathers will be edged in grey, while males will have solid red feathers and the males also have a very thin white stripe on edge.

1. The parrot's diet

A balanced and rational diet will insure a permanent healthy state for your bird.

The main diet of Senegal parrots should consist of high-quality pellets or a high quality mixture of seeds (millet, oat, hemp, wheat, etc....); supplemented with fresh fruits and vegetables, daily. There is another option for a main 100% healthy diet, like a mix of sprouted grains and seeds, raw and boiled veggies, fruits and a few good quality pellets.

Pellets are a blend of vegetables, fruits, grains, seeds, and protein. They are baked and then formed into shapes and sizes for different species. You should always check the package for feeding instructions on pellets. The bigger your bird, the bigger the pellets should be. Senegal parrots like African Grey Parrots need more calcium intake than other parrot species. Calcium deficiency is common in captive Senegal parrots, especially in birds who may have been fed only on seeds and because of the lack of the natural sunlight. Try to expose your bird to natural sunlight as much as possible, and you must assure a calcium-rich diet for your bird, daily. You can offer them calcium-rich vegetables and fruits like broccoli, carrots, spinach, dandelion greens, mustard greens, figs, kale, endive and apricots. There are specially prepared parrot foods in stores, which contain calcium.

In the wild, Senegal parrots eat seeds, grains, plants, nuts, some insects, buds, flowers, berries, they also like to raid maize and millet fields.

Senegal parrots are very likely to gain weight, so owners should monitor their fat intake. Overfeeding leads to selective feeding and wasteful throwing of food. Millet, especially spray millet a good treat food.

You can mix some cooked brown rice with broccoli, kale, spinach, peppers, dandelion leaves and cooked sweet potatoes. Cereals like wheat contain a high level of sulphur, which can be administered to your parrot as a food supplement in the molting period. The sulphur helps to regenerate the plumage of the bird, that`s why you need to increase the quantity of wheat in your parrot's diet during molting period. Oat seeds contain carbohydrates and a high level of albumins, which have an important role in the development of young parrots. Adult parrots should have only 10% of supplementation in their diet from this cereal because too much oat can lead to obesity.

Corn seeds contain a low level of vitamins and albumins but are very rich in carbohydrates. Senegal parrots love to eat boiled corn so that you can offer them as treats. Small seeds like millet and canary seeds should be mixed with the Senegal's regular seed mix, but be careful as too much millet seeds offered as treats could lead to obesity. Canary seeds contain carbohydrates. Fruits contain sugar, which has very low quantities of nutrients.

If you don't have enough time to offer your bird a fresh diet variety every day, and you choose to feed your bird mostly with pellets, then you'll have to keep in mind that good quality pellets must represent between 60-80 % of your parrot's diet.

It's better to give your bird more pellets than seeds because pellets offer a complete nutrition.

Senegal parrots which were fed only seeds used to have a shorter lifespan because seeds contain a high level of fat and insufficient vitamins, proteins and minerals.

Seeds have to represent no more than 12% of your parrot's diet, and they must not be dusty, or mold infested: hemp seeds, flax, sunflower, safflower, niger, canary grass, white millet, canola, etc.

Grains: rice, alfalfa, triticale, buckwheat, sesame, amaranth, quinoa.

If you decide to feed your bird with a 100% healthy diet, like sprouted seeds and grains, raw and boiled veggies, fruits and a few pellets, then mix all of the ingredients in one dish. A half a cup of this mix is enough for a day period. Sprouted seeds and grains provide nutrient-rich food, are lower in fat and will help balance your parrot's diet.

If the weather is too cold for sprouting, the seeds and grains can be boiled for about 30 minutes instead of sprouting them.

Sprouted seeds and grains are also good in the weaning period for youngsters because the softened shell is easier to break and the young birds can get used to the texture of seeds.

Nuts and hazelnuts should be given in the same quantity as the seeds, and have to be offered in their shell because it can be a good brain exercise for your bird. Almond, cashew, pecan, pistachio, walnut etc. can be given to your parrot. If you have a young bird, you should teach him/her how to do it, by cracking the hazelnut shell. You can offer your bird rice bread and rye bread; cereals like oat flakes or corn flakes but without sugar, for example.

You can also make healthy homemade bird treats. For this, you will need oats, your basic birdseeds, flour, honey, water and millet.

In a plastic bowl add 2 tablespoons of oats, 2 tablespoons of bird seeds, 1 tablespoon of flour, 1 teaspoon of millets, then add half of a tablespoon of water and give it a quick mix. After that, add 1 tablespoon of honey and mix until it is fully incorporated. Add more water if it is necessary. Then roll them into small balls and put them on the baking sheet. Put them in the oven for 30 minutes at 180 degrees Celsius (356 degrees Fahrenheit).

During winter you can offer your bird soft food, for example, bread that was previously softened in milk and then mixed with some grated carrots, calcium and minced berries of sea-buckthorn (Hippophae rhamnoides). Vegetables are very good nutrients for your bird; frozen veggies are just as nutritious as fresh veggies. During summer you can offer them fresh veggies: cucumbers, tomatoes, broccoli, cauliflowers, carrots, green beans, pod peas, lettuce, dark leafy greens, peppers, celery, zucchini, etc... Vegetables should be given in higher quantities than fruits.

Dried veggies and fruits are also good options for your bird. Senegal parrots toss dried fruits and veggies into the water bowl and then eat them, once they are rehydrated. You can leave the dried veggies and fruits in the bird`s cage for days unless they get wet. Try to avoid purchasing dried veggies and fruits that contain preservatives, like sulphur dioxide. Senegal parrots also love fresh fruits like grapes, melon, bananas, pears, nectarines, pineapple, apple dices, cactus fruits, figs, pomegranate, peaches, kiwi, papayas, mango dices, strawberries, cranberries, blueberries, grapefruit, oranges, cherries, etc... You don't need to peel oranges, tangerines, and grapefruits because your bird will love doing it himself. Bee pollen granules, banana, and coconut chips are also some of the favorite foods of the Senegal parrot. You can also offer fresh herbs like yarrow (Achillea millefolium), plantain (Plantago lanceolata), coltsfoot (Tussilago farfara), shepherd's purse (Capsella bursa pastoris), dandelion (Taraxacum officinale), red clover (Trifolium), red raspberry leaf, basil leaf, etc. Leaves and branches of fruit trees, oak trees, beech trees (Fagus sylvatica) and willow trees (Salix alba) are the best source of vitamins; you can provide them directly from forests. You also have to offer the opportunity to your parrot to chew these kind of branches.

Offer your bird boiled eggs once or twice per week. Boiled egg shells are the best source of calcium so that you can offer them to your bird in crushed form. Your parrot will love to eat some boiled chicken, beef and fish once or twice per week. Occasionally, you can give them cooked meat bones.

When your bird is eating fruits, its droppings become more watery, but this should not cause alarm. Senegal parrots which are fed on high-quality pellets usually don't need vitamin and mineral supplementation. Over-supplementation with vitamins could lead to the intoxication of your bird. Supplementation with vitamins is recommended just in case when your bird's main diet is based on seeds.

Another important thing is, never give up when you try to offer your bird new foods and it refuses them. You'll have to try more than once, by mixing the new food into other foods. Birds learn by observation, and they watch what we eat so that they will try the new food. Human table food like scrambled eggs and pasta are permitted if fed in small portions. Avoid giving your bird avocado, chocolate, caffeine, sugary or salty snacks, milk products and alcohol! Uneaten food should be removed from the cages after two hours. It's very important to have some grit in the cage also.

Next, I will present three parrot mash recipes. You will need: 1 cup of beans, 2 cups of grains, 2-3 carrots, 1 yellow, 1 red, 1 orange pepper, 1 cauliflower, 1 broccoli, dark green leafy vegetables (dark green lettuces, cabbage, kale, Italian parsley, broccoli green leaves, spinach, dandelion leaves, etc....), 2 apples, a half melon, 1 banana and 6 strawberries.

Separately soak the grains and beans for about 6 hours each. Rinse each and add purified water (don't use tap water) until the beans and grains are slightly covered. Both beans and grains will soak up water, so be sure to cover them with extra water. During soaking, the beans will double in size and grains swell slightly. Boil for 15 minutes uncovered, then cover and simmer for another 15 minutes. Let cool and mix beans and grains.

Mix the chopped vegetables and dark leafy greens with the food processor and add some water.

Then mix together the chopped apples (avoid seeds), melon, banana and strawberries.

Combine equal parts of the vegetable-green mix with bean-grain mix and then add 1 cup of fruit mix for every 6 cups of the above. Mix together and then put in safe freezer containers and freeze. Thaw for 24 hours in the refrigerator before use. Do not use a microwave to thaw.

For the second recipe of parrot mash you will need:

½ cooked sweet potato, 4-5 teaspoons of fully cooked grains (oats, quinoa seeds, brown rice, wheat, rye), 2 teaspoons of chopped veggies (cauliflower, broccoli, red, orange, yellow peppers, carrot, zucchini, etc....), 1 teaspoon of unsweetened applesauce.

With a fork, mash ½ cooked the sweet potato and mixed with 4-5 teaspoon of fully cooked grains. If it is too dry, then you can add a little water. You can also add 1 teaspoon of unsweetened applesauce and mix.

The third one is "Sweet potato balls" and for this recipe, you will need:

1 cooked sweet potato, 1 mashed banana, ½ cup raisins, 1 cup mixed fresh or frozen vegetables (celery; carrots; red, yellow, orange peppers; zucchini; broccoli; cauliflower; green peas; etc....), 1 cup diced apples, 1 and ½ cup uncooked oatmeal and corn flakes.

Mix all together and add some fruit juice to make it form small balls. You'll have to freeze balls individually. Defrost them before serving.

When you purchase your bird, you have to know all about your bird's diet: what kind of food s/he has previously consumed. If the bird has not received the proper diet, then you have to replace it gradually. You'll need to offer your newly arrived bird freshwater and pieces of apples. If your bird presents signs of weakness, you'll have to offer some moist biscuits and egg paste; if s/he looks healthy, you can give your bird the usual food, but you can also add in his/her food some poppy seeds (it will have a calming effect on your bird). Chamomile tea (instead of water) also has a good calming effect and makes your bird feel more relaxed.

The right owner for a Senegal parrot has to be somebody who wants to invest time in it, and for this reason, before you get a parrot, you have to study these birds' behavior and learn about the requirements to look after them. The most important thing that you have to do is to get your bird used to other people. You have to make sure that almost every day your parrot will have the chance to get in contact with new people, to experience new surroundings. All those experiences and interactions with other people must be a positive experience for them.

If you want to teach your parrot to talk, then you'll have to be more patient, you'll have to speak very often with him/her, and your voice has to be very calm. The training lessons have to represent positive experiences for your parrot, and they have to last for about 5-10 minutes, once or twice a day. It could be one hour after the bird wakes up and about one hour before the bird goes to sleep, that`s because during the day the bird is most active and when they are active they`re less inclined to be open to training.

You have to combine training time with playtime because you want to make the bird enjoy the training because they deal with a positive experience.

You'll have to encourage your parrot with the right words like "well done, " and you'll have to offer rewards every time s/he says the words right.

Be aware, never yell or hurt your parrot when s/he doing something wrong or you feel that s/he is stressing you. The bird will lose its confidence in you and it will be very hard for you to retrain it again. For the first days, don't try to handle the bird, because the most important thing is to get used to each other.

Place the cage in the room where you spend the most time. Talk to your bird as much as possible and when you change the water and food, try to do it by not stressing the bird too much. After a few days, you can leave the cage door open, and s/he will realize that you are the best friend for him/her. S/he will come out of the cage and will learn to step up on your finger. Soon you will observe that your parrot will sit very comfortably on your shoulder, which means that s/he accepted you.

Parrots, in general, love sitting on people's shoulders and love to chew things which decreases their aggression and actual depression problems. They like to chew on your hair; you don't have to worry about it (they don't bite it off), they're just chewing on it because they're enjoying that.

One of the most important words for your parrot to learn is "step up." Even if s/he steps up on your finger without any previous command, it is recommended to say the words "step up" every time the bird is performing your command, and you'll have to say: "well done," "good girl" or "good boy" after that.

Some parrots do learn to talk very well, but first, they learn to talk on their own, by listening to human conversations and imitating sounds. So, the first thing you can do to encourage your parrot to talk is to repeat the words all the time. To encourage your parrot to say specific phrases that you want your parrot to repeat, try to say them on a regular basis. Talk to your parrot when s/he is concentrated on you, that is usually when his/her eyes are attentive.

The first word that most parrots will learn is "Hello" because that is the first thing they hear whenever someone walks into a room.

It's very important to reward and to answer to your parrot every time it's saying words or making sounds, even if they are not correct. Don't scream at your bird when s/he is very loud; you better try to maintain a calm conversation. Watch out what you say in front of your bird, parrots learn the words that you don't want them to learn very quickly.

Senegal parrots are shyer and they tend to talk in their cages. Meanwhile, other species of parrots like Cockatoos and Amazons love attention.

You can use clickers with success to achieve the best training results; parrots usually learn quicker when you're using a clicker. When you start training your bird, first give it a treat and at the same time say "well done" or click the clicker. Your parrot will associate these sounds with the treat. Once the bird makes the association between praise (click) and treat, you can delay the reward. If your parrot already knows the "step up" command, then it's easy to teach him/her to say "hello." You'll have to raise your hand in front of the bird, just like you want the bird to step up on it. When s/he steps up say "well done" and give to your bird the treat. Repeat this command for a few times, until the bird will understand it. Once the bird has raised his/her leg on its own to get the treat, wait and give the treat only when the bird is raising its leg a little bit higher. You can also use very subtle signs with your hands if you want your parrot to answer back to you. You have to choose a sign and use it in the same way you use a command, followed by a treat or praise. Your bird will learn every little movement of your fingers.

Teach your parrot to play basketball, using a miniature-sized basketball hoop by picking up "an easy to hold ball" and passing it through the tiny basket. Show your bird the basketball and say

"Toss!" and then put the basketball through the hoop. Next, hand the ball to your bird and say "Toss!" If your bird puts the ball through the hoop, say "Well done!" in a happy, excited tone.

Rope climbing exercise

For this exercise you will need a cotton rope (about 2.5-3 meters long), make knots in it about every 15 cm.

Attach the rope from the ceiling using a metal hook. Place the parrot on the floor at the end of the rope and say, "Climb the rope!"

If your parrot doesn't want to climb upward on the rope, then you will have to hold a treat at 20 cm above the bird, and gradually move the treat towards the top end of the rope. As soon as your bird gets to the top knot, say, "Well done!" and at the same time give it the treat. You can repeat this exercise 5-6 times in one session. If your parrot already knows how to perform the exercise, you can replace the treats with lots of encouraging words.

How to train parrots to stop biting

When parrots feel threatened, they will react in different ways, like screaming, flapping their wings, running away, growling, hissing, biting, etc...

Several factors can make parrots feel threatened like, perturbing them when attention is not wanted, invading their territory, sudden movements, unexpected noises and jealousy. Parrots can also bite when protecting their mate. If your bird has chosen you as a mate, it may feel that unfamiliar persons or new pets appear as a threat to your safety. In these situations it is best to gradually introduce your bird to the new person or pet, allowing your bird enough time to accept the change.

Parrots who are going through hormonal changes during the breeding season or molting may become annoyed and moody, which may lead to biting. You should watch your bird's body language during these periods and leave your bird alone when attention is not wanted. It`s our natural behavior when a bird bites, to put the bird down and then we start to yell at that bird. In this situation, we reinforce the bird to bite us, because that brings the bird more and more attention.

When your young parrot tries to nibble on your ears, fingers or other body parts you should offer them an acceptable alternative to chew on: apple slice, carrot, a block of wood, etc.… If the method above doesn't work, then gently blow in their face and in a firm voice tell them "no".

All we want to do is to reinforce and reward good behaviors like doing interactive things, standing on your hand, playing quietly, that is positive and socially acceptable.

For example, choose a toy, a key or an object which could interest your parrot, when s/he is touching that object reward or praise your bird. After s/he seems to look that s/he understands that command, make it pick up that object. You have to repeat this game until your parrot will pick it up and will bring you that object.

Training lessons have to be short; about 5-10 minutes and to represent a positive experience for you and your bird.

The rewards (treats) have to be in small quantities, but also something that your bird will enjoy to eat, like sunflower seeds, for example. If you offer big rewards to your bird, then s/he will spend too much time eating them, and your training lesson will be interrupted for too long.

If your bird bites you, try hard not to even yell out in pain, just take the bird and put it down and walk away. Your parrot will learn, that when s/he bites you, then s/he will lose your attention.

Make sure your bird has things available to play with, so that s/he will not bite you. Your parrot can't shred toys and bite at the same time, so if you can anticipate the behavior happening, regardless of what the behavior is (biting, screaming), you can provide some distraction for your bird.

You can place a wooden chopstick within the bird`s reach. When the bird bites the stick, you should praise it. After all, your bird will understand that biting a stick is a good thing.

Learn to observe your parrot`s body language

Parrots usually show us how they're feeling and what they're going to do, by using their bodies in different ways.

When they have their tail flared it means that they are excited or they will bite you. If your parrot has all its feathers sticking out, with its wings held out from the body, then s/he could be ready to fight.

You can also observe a few clues from your parrot when s/he intends to bite. It will open its beak and will spread its legs apart for a firmer grip on the perch. You can interact with your parrot to prevent the bite when you observe these kinds of signs.

When your parrot is happy to see a friend of yours or another bird, then s/he might puff out all its feathers or wag its tail or move its beak up and down, stretch one wing and one leg together out from the side of the body.

Senegal parrots learn to amuse themselves, by playing tricks on some people with their body language, by giving outward signs of friendliness, and then they will bite when they're approached with fingers.

They do such things because they like to test people and see if they will jump away.

Chapter 4: Cold season, hot season

1. **How to care for your bird in cold season**

Exotic birds can't handle sudden weather changes (from sudden cold to sudden hot weather), you'll have to maintain a constant temperature for them during winter. Parrots like humidity, so if the air condition of your house is very dry, because of the heating system, it is recommended to spray your bird daily with a handheld spray bottle.

2. **How to care for your bird in hot season**

Many people think that parrots feel at "home" in high temperatures, but bird owners have to be prepared for hot weather. A bird's body temperature is between 104-105.8 degrees Fahrenheit (40-41 degrees Celsius). Therefore, your bird will withstand temperatures that go up to this level. Birds don't have sweat glands as we do, so they can't adjust their body temperature. When we perspire, the evaporation of the moisture on our skin cools us. There are several ways in which your bird can drop its body temperature:

- Heat loss during panting: birds increase their breathing rate, by faster breathing with the beak open. They have dry mouths, and while we see them panting, when they're overheated, they're reacting to the heat, and this does not mean that they can combat it without our help. Their life could be in danger because they can become dehydrated by evaporation of the water through respiratory system (mouth, nostrils, and lungs).

- evaporation of water through skin and feet

- through the vibration of the neck structures.

Birds that are brought outside should be watched closely. If you observe that your parrot is holding its wings away from its body and is panting, then you have to bring it to cooler temperatures and shower it with water at room temperature. Using cold water on the overheated bird can cause organ damage, shock and even death.

Don't place the cage in direct sunlight, because your bird will need a shady place with humidity. You can attach a spray or sprinkler system to the top of the cage or of your aviary and you can also set a timer on, and cool down the cages to offer your bird a refreshing shower.

3. Cleaning your bird's house

Your beloved parrot could be easily affected by the bacteria which can live in the cage during the day, that's why you need to clean it every day and a more complex clean every week. The floor of the cage, the food and water recipients should be cleaned daily.

I recommend that the floor of the cage should be covered with kitchen towel or paper sheets, which can be changed daily. The disinfection of the cage, food and water recipients must be cleaned with hot water weekly.

Don't use disinfection products very often because they are toxic to your parrot! When you do so, be careful and move the bird in a different room. It's very important to use eye protection glasses and gloves when the disinfection operation is taking place because it can cause serious injuries.

You can use bleach for disinfection, but be aware not to mix it with other chemical products, because it's very dangerous. You can use the bleach in the diluted form: 30 ml of bleach mixed with 250ml of water. This mixture will be very efficient to combat bacteria and viruses. After you finish the disinfection process, it's very important to rinse the recipients and the cage.

4. Cages and accessories

When you choose a cage for your bird, you have to take into consideration the size and the temperament of your bird, because s/he will spend almost all its time in that cage.

You have to be sure that your bird will be able to fly without any problem between the climbing perches or to flap its wings.

Cage location

Your parrot just adores when you are around him/her, so you'll have to place the cage in the same room where you spend most of your time. To avoid any possible danger, you'll have to take into consideration a few aspects:

- place the cage near the window, so your parrot can enjoy the natural light;

- avoid placing the cage in air currents;

- avoid placing the cage in the kitchen, especially when you cook, because the steam contains toxic substances;

- don't place the cage near a television or near any home audio system.

Cages

The cage has to be two or three times bigger than the bird's wingspan and three times bigger than the bird's length from head to tail. It has to be big enough for the bird, so it will be able to open its wings and flap them. Especially for single birds, you'll have to equip the cage with toys, mirrors, and swings.

You'll have to change the toys very often, to keep your bird from becoming bored. To maintain your parrot's feet, you must provide proper perches for the bird's feet. Otherwise, it will be difficult for your parrot to hold on to a perch properly. Your parrot should be able to stand on the perch, without the toes completely touching each other in a circle.

If you choose to offer your parrot natural branch perches, make sure that they are without any wild bird droppings and free of insects. You'll have to disinfect it with hot boiled water before using it. There are also comfortable braided rope perches, which are a good choice for your bird to rest on. Grooming perches will keep your bird's beak in shape.

The resistance of the cage is very important, one made of metal is much more resistant than one made of plastic. The space between the bars is very important because the bird could get its head, legs or even its beak stuck. When you buy a cage make sure that it's not painted, because parrots will eat the paint, and if the paint is toxic, s/he can get sick and even die. The size of the cage has to be around 47.1 x 47.1 x 47.1 inches. The cage should be in a corner or against the wall to give a feeling of security.

The nesting box should be at the highest point of the cage, and the entrance hole should be in a shaded position. A ladder must be fixed inside just below the entrance hole to allow access up and down the box.

Aviaries

Outdoor aviaries are more spacious than traditional cages and what's more important is that they allow parrots more space and offer a natural environment and fresh air.

An outdoor housing place is made up of two compartments: a net aviary (flight unit) and a sheltered place.

The net aviary has to be made of galvanized steel mesh, and it should be 19 gauges (19G) and maximum dimension of 2.5 cm x 1.25 cm (1 x ½ in). Netting of this size should also help to keep rodents and snakes out of the aviary; these creatures may well eat the eggs and the birds as well. To protect the aviary from predators like rats, weasels, and cats you need to bury the galvanized wire mesh deeply (at least a foot) in the ground, or you will need to lay down a solid base, constructed using blocks or bricks sunken into the ground. Ideally, the floor of the flight should be of concrete, which is much easier to clean than grass. The aviary should have provisions for food, drinking water, bathing water, grit, perching, nesting and a place to hang a Cuttlefish bone. During the day your Senegal parrot will perch on twigs or wooden dowels, and you can offer your bird pinecones, balls or chains to play with. If you place potted plants in your aviary, the birds will spend a lot of time perching, picking and climbing, so you should provide nonpoisonous plants like a fruit tree, a honeysuckle bush or a forsythia.

The dimensions of the flight are 4-5 meters in length (157,4 - 196,8 inches); up to 2 meters in height (78.74 inches); and between 1.2 and 1.8 meters wide (70,86 inches) width.

The perches should never be so thick that your birds cannot grip them adequately, nor so thin that the bird's front toes curl right round to the back. Perches can be constructed in the shape of a `T`, and fixed in the floor, or suspended using wire loops attached firmly to the aviary framework. Perches should not overhang feeding utensils because these are likely to be soiled by droppings from above. None of the wood used for perches should have been recently sprayed with chemicals. Branches are sometimes soiled by other wild birds, so it`s very important to wash them before use. In southern states of USA, outdoor caging must be protected from opossums to prevent exposure to the parasite called Sarcocystis Falcatula, which can result in a fatal lung infection.

Roofing

The roof of the flight nearest to the shelter should be covered with translucent plastic sheeting. This will help the birds to sit outside when the weather is bad, or it`s very hot. The shelter can be roofed with marine plywood, with all the cracks being filled with a waterproofing material and tarred over before heavy-duty roofing felt is applied. This should overlap for several inches down the sides of the shelter. To ensure that the interior remains dry, guttering should be attached along the back of the sloping roof, to carry the rainwater away from the aviary. Those kept in colder climates may need a heated, sheltered area as they are susceptible to chilling and frostbitten toes.

5. Toys and accessories

Very inventive and always searching for something new, Senegal parrots will be happy to find all kind of toys in their cages.

You have to be careful when you choose the toys because Senegal parrots tend to take apart things, because every new toy is a challenge for them. When you choose toys for your parrot it is like choosing toys for a child: they have to be safe, and the bird has to be happy to play with them without stressing itself.

The best toys for them are pieces of softwood or perches, ping-pong balls, all kind of unpainted paper-made items, etc.... You'll have to provide some items which help to maintain the physical health condition of your bird:

  - acrylic toys with bells attached

  - swings and chains which increases the capacity of movement;

  - therapeutic perches which help to maintain the bird's feet;

  - perches or any wooden objects which are good for chewing (if you neglect your bird by not offering him/her different objects to chew, this could lead to beak deformation);

  - a bowl of fresh water for a bath;

  - Various nutritional supplements like Cuttlefish bone, seashells, etc....

One of the best games that your parrot could play is when s/he has to get out a peanut which was previously hidden inside of a tiny hole of a log. Your parrot has to chew the log to get inside and to get the peanut. This game makes your bird concentrate and to work hard to eat.

You can also make your parrot happy by replacing the old toys and perches with new ones. In fact, toys and interactive games which make your bird work hard mentally and physically will keep your bird healthy and svelte.

Chapter 5: How to maintain your parrot's health

The first sign of disease

There are several physical and behavioral signs of the bird's illness:

- depressed attitude and unusual irritability;
- they sleep more than 10-12 hours per day, with their head hidden under the wing;
- they keep their eyes almost shut all the time, and the wings hang from the body;
- don't have the same stability on their legs and they spend more time than usual on the bottom of the cage;
- their appetite is reduced, and they are losing weight;
- don't clean their plumage and their feet;
- An excessive cough and sneeze and nose secretion dripping;
- the feathers around the beak are dirty;
- their feces color differs from normal, and they present diarrhea;
- excessive molting;
- discoloration of the feathers;
- breathing difficulties.

When you recognize these signs, you should contact your vet doctor for a precise diagnosis.

The most important condition to keep your birds healthy is a proper diet. Choosing the appropriate cage and the right environment are very important factors. A smaller cage than usual can cause agitation, and the bird will try to escape.

The cage must be kept clean, to avoid bacterial infestation. Daily flying exercises are needed.

Watch out for your ornamental plants: philodendron, iris and yellow daffodil could be poisonous for your birds. Cigarette smoke, hairspray (hair lacquer), body spray, furniture spray and vapors of household cleaners like bleach should be avoided when the birds are around. Avoid exposing your cage with your parrot outside when there are cats around because they can easily knock down the cage.

Learn about the natural habits of your bird, for example, you can find out if your birds love to have a bath more often than showers, then you have to place a bowl filled with water in the cage, or for the other option you'll have to spray him/her with water very often. Try to discover and offer your bird the most favorite and natural foods as possible and make natural environments for it.

Have regular veterinary examinations, because birds can hide the signs of diseases. In the wild, sick birds hide any sign of their disease, they even try to eat with the rest of the flock, because there is a risk that the others will steal his food and bite him because they feel his weakness. The cage birds can act the same way; they look like they are healthy, they eat very well, until one day they fall off from the perches. Even when they have sharp pains, they don't tend to exteriorize their feelings. The bird's plumage can hide the eventual weight loss caused by diseases.

If you recognize the signs presented above, you better visit your avian vet as soon as possible. Sometimes a routine examination can help to discover any latent infection of the bird.

1.   How to recognize abnormal droppings

Your bird eliminates feces and urine at the same time. The color of feces depends on the assimilation of the food, and it can vary from dark green and brown to black. On the feces there is a white urine patch. If the darker part of the feces is more liquid, then the bird has diarrhea. When the urine appears like a lake around the fecal material, there could be kidney problems. There could be situations when you have to visit your avian vet for routine examinations (check-ups), and because of the stress, the droppings of your bird could have a very liquid form, but just for a short period and it will normally pass. For a precise examination, you better visit your avian vet.

2.   Feather picking and self-mutilation

When a bird moves its beak through the feathers making them clean, then this is preening. But when the bird starts to pay too much attention to its feathers by pulling them out obsessively, then this is self-mutilation.

There could be several causes of this problem like skin diseases, stress or internal diseases. When the main cause is the skin itchiness, among the special treatments prescribed by your avian vet, you can also apply some anesthetic powder directly to the bird's skin. In this period you'll have to avoid placing the cage near radiators or in direct sunlight because the bird's skin will become excessively dry.

3.   How to catch and manipulate your parrot without hurting it

There are many situations when you'll have to catch and hold the bird in your hands. First of all, you have to remove all the accessories from the cage, including the water and feeding bowls, the mirror and other things. The easiest method to catch the bird without stressing it is to turn the power off in the room where the bird is located. Before you turn the power off, you'll have to know exactly where the bird is located. You can catch him/her very easy because s/he can`t see very well in the dark. You can also use a scarf by placing it on the head of your parrot to be able to grab the neck then to fix the head. With the other hand, you'll have to hold the legs with which s/he can cause serious injuries. For this procedure, you'll have to use some leather gloves. It is better to grab them by the neck than by the belly because a parrot`s neck is extremely strong, flexible and mobile, and it has more vertebrae than humans or mammals. The neck is considered to be the strongest part of a parrot`s body.

Birds breathe by expanding the rib cage outward, which draws air in. That`s why is so important when you examine or try to clip your bird's wings to avoid pressing the chest area because it will not be able to breathe. They have a very strong beak and neck so they can hang on your fingers without any problem. When you are carrying them around restrained you can hold them on their back, this is also useful for when you need to groom your parrot or check its wings. For the examination of the bird, you need two people present: one to hold the bird and one for the examination: Check both wings of the bird, first by opening the left and then the right wing like a fan and check the feathers. With a magnifying glass, you can check for ticks. You can also check the breast muscle by touching it very gently. In the middle part of the chest, there is the sternum. If you feel that the stern is very sharp, then it could be malnutrition (the bird is sick for a longer period or doesn't receive enough food).

You can also check the cloacal opening, the common orifice through which the feces and urine are eliminated, and in females, the eggs pass just through the same opening. The feathers from this area must be clean, if they are not, it means that the bird suffers from diarrhea. You'll have to check the belly, which is under the stern, by pressing it very gently. It normally has to be soft and flat, if it's bumped over the stern level and it's firm, then there could be a sign of a tumor.

Eczemas or injuries can be found easily if you blow some air under the feathers and you can check for any injuries or lumps on the bird's skin. You can check for abscesses on the feet, which can be uncomfortable for your bird.

4. How to choose the right avian vet

The best way to choose the right avian vet is by asking your friends, who already own birds for a longer period. When you call the vet, ask him if he is a bird expert.

Before visiting your vet, you have to be prepared with some information about your bird. You have to know your bird`s age, if not, an experienced vet will help you with this.

The vet will ask you a few questions like:

How long have you owned the bird?
Where are they from?
Do you have any other pets?
Did you buy another bird?
Are there health problems in your family?
When did the symptoms appear and what are they?
Was the bird treated before by you or by another vet?
What kind of food do you give to the bird?
Did the bird participate in exhibition shows?

It's very important to visit the same vet every time your bird presents health problems because this way he can follow the bird's evolution.

5.   Microchipping your parrot

A microchip is a very small electronic device encased in a glass chamber, about the size of a rice grain, which is inserted into a bird. When a scanner is passed over the area of the body containing the chip, it is activated, and it transmits an identification number and the name of the chip manufacturer to the scanner's display screen. The person scanning, using the manufacturer database, will locate the contact information of the owner. Make sure the scanned microchip number matches with the number on the computerized paper strip that goes in the brochure which the client takes home.

You can also ask your avian vet to check the proper functioning of the microchip periodically. The microchip is implanted (on the left side) into the pectoral muscle of the bird or under the wings. The procedure is much like an injection, and it lasts about 10 seconds; the chip is implanted through a hypodermic needle. It can be done without the use of anesthetics, but many vets prefer to anesthetize to ensure proper placement. If you are changing your address and phone number, don't forget to announce to your vet or specialist from the animal shelter to register your new address. Microchips are not GPS devices; they're to identify found birds. Birds which are found and taken to animal shelters are scanned for microchips before they're adopted. It is recommended that you use a widely known brand increasing the probability that a scanner for that brand is available.

Inflammation of the skin (Dermatitis)

Inflammation of the skin could appear among other diseases, like renal diseases, with increasing levels of uric acid in the blood, liver disease or infestation with external parasites.

You can use the following therapeutic measures:

- Applying astringent and disinfectant solution on the wet wounds. Do not use ointments, because the feathers will become greasy and the bird will peck the wounds.

- There are injections with antibiotics, which stop the bacterial infestations. Injections with multivitamins and immune system boosters can help the bird to fight against diseases.

- In case that there are itchiness problems, it would be recommended to use some special anesthetic powder for external use on the affected areas on the skin. In this case, the skin will be anesthetized, and the itchiness should disappear.

- When there is the possibility of massive bleedings (because the bird is scratching too much) a collar should be applied around the bird's neck. In some cases, the bird won't be happy to support the collar, especially if the itchiness was caused by physical problems (stress), and maybe this solution (collar) will not resolve the problem.

Skin tumors (Lipomas)

Skin tumors can appear in all species of birds. The most common tumors are lipomas which are fatty tumors that can develop beneath the skin, and could appear on the stomach or chest area, it also can develop internally.

A common cause of lipomas is obesity and vitamin E deficiency. The proper treatment is a low-fat diet. If the lipoma is big and painful or infected, your vet will surgically remove the tumor, because this is the best option for your bird's health.

Parasites

External parasites

External parasites or ectoparasites can be divided into lice, mites and the rest. Lice infestations appear as small, brownish colored insects that can be seen moving through your bird's feathers. Sometimes you can't see lice with the naked eye, you just simply notice excessive itching in your bird.

Parrot lice lay their eggs at the base of the feather and the egg developing period could take up to 6 weeks. The most common mite seen on birds is Cnemidocoptes - the Scaly Face / Leg mite, which feeds on keratin, the protein that makes up the surface layer of the skin, beak, and feet. Left untreated, the Scaly Face mite can disrupt the growth areas of the beak, leading to distortion of the beak.

The depluming itch mite (Cnemidocoptes gallinae)

It`s a microscopic Sarcoptidae mite which can be found between live feather brushes and tail feathers (cloaca), thigh, abdomen head and neck area.

Confirmation of parasites infestation can be made after a parasitological examination. Infestation with these types of parasites is more frequent during spring and summer.

Symptoms: weight loss, feather scratching and pecking, inflamed skin, the infested birds bite themselves and may pull out their feathers.

Treatments: Pyrethrum based powders. Carbaryl, Cypermethrin, Deltamethrin, Flumethrin, Neguvon, Ectomin, Neostomosan (tetramethrin).

Scaly Leg mite (Cnemidocoptes mutans)

It usually appears in adult birds. The evolution of the disease is very slow; it could be observed after 6-12 months. The lesions appear on the legs. The parasite burrows under the scales of the bird's legs or feet forming crusts. At first, the crust is thin; then it will become thicker. Thickening of the scales on the legs can lead to pain. You can soak the bird's feet and legs in warm water, then gently dry them with a towel. Try to remove the dead, loose scales with a toothbrush gently. Then you'll have to dip the feet and legs in glycerin, vegetable, olive or linseed oil to suffocate the parasites. Wipe off the oil from the feet and apply some petroleum jelly. The treatment has to be done twice per day until the skin becomes very soft and you will able to exfoliate it. It may take several months to resolve the problem.

In case of massive infestation, total or partial loss of feathering will appear.

The combat of parasites can also be done with treatments with Ivermectin or Moxidectin, which can be applied to the skin on the back of the neck or mixed in the bird's drinking water.

Dermanyssus gallinae, the red bird mite, appears mostly in aviary birds and does not live on the bird's body. During the day, they are hiding in cracks and crevices around aviaries. Massive infestation takes place during summer.

You'll notice that your bird will refuse to sleep on the perches, this could happen because of the mites. The treatment must be done with insecticides in the aviary, nesting boxes, and perches, before the birds were previously moved, after disinfection you need to rinse the disinfected tools with water.

The birds will be treated with powder which contains Pyrethrum. Decontamination will be repeated after 7 days.

The air sac mites (Cytodites nudus)

Cytokines nudus mites are localized in the air sacs, bronchial passages, and lungs, in cavities of the bones, liver and kidneys. When the mites infest the lungs, they may cause granulomatous pneumonia. It could infest chickens, turkeys, pheasants, pigeons, canaries, parrots, etc.... These mites lay their eggs in the inferior part of the respiratory system, then they are eliminated through feces. Contamination could happen through infested drinking water. The mites are spread by respiratory mucus. In heavy infestation, the affected birds present cough, anemia, anorexia, asphyxiation crisis, lethargy and dyspnoea. In these stages, the sick birds could die. Making any diagnosis other than by autopsy is difficult.

Treatments: Ivermectin in drinking water. Prevention of further cases is made by the administration of Malathion with aerosol. A rigorous disinfection of the cage or aviary is required.

Internal parasites

Gapeworm (Syngamus Trachea)

It`s a disease caused by a worm called Syngamus trachea, which is located in the trachea of the affected bird. The gapeworm also affects turkeys, geese, cage birds and wild birds, especially wild pheasants. Infestation occurs when there are wild pheasants close to your birds or indirectly by intermediate hosts like earthworms and snails.

Gapeworms are located in the trachea, bronchi and the lungs. Gurgling noises that come from the throat of the bird are caused by the gapeworm infestation, and it can be confused with respiratory problems.

Symptoms: difficult breathing with open beak, cough, anemia, anorexia and weakness; if there is a heavy infestation with gapeworms, then the bird could die by suffocation.

Treatments: Thiabendazole powder in feed. Fenbendazole (Panacur) for 3 days. Flubendazole for youngsters in feed for 7 days. Febantel (Rental) in feed for 7 days. Tetramisole-Nilverm administered in water for 3 days. Disinfection and dry maintenance of the aviary or cage are required.

Trichomoniasis (Trichomonas gallinae)

This parasite is located in the sinuses, mouth, throat, crop, intestine, and liver of the bird. Among domestic birds, there are also wild birds which are infested with this kind of internal parasite (sparrows, vultures, seagulls, wild doves, etc....).

Symptoms: white or yellow cheesy-looking nodules inside of the mouth and throat; reduced appetite; excessive mucus in the mouth, esophagus, and crop, vomiting, dehydration, weight loss, respiratory disorders and even death.

Treatments: you must gently remove the cheesy deposits from the bird's mouth and apply some tincture of glycerin-iodine solution (1%trypaflavine).

Dimetridazole for 3-5 days or Metronidazole (Flagyl) twice daily for 5-6 days or Ronidazole for 7 days.

You must separate the infected birds from the others.

Histomoniasis

It's caused by parasites (Histomonas meleagridis) which affect the ceca and the liver of the bird. The youngsters are more exposed to this kind of infection.

Symptoms: excrements of yellow color, walking disorders caused by the inflammation of the joints.

Treatments: administration of Dimetridazole; Ronidazole; polivitamines.

It can be prevented by the disinfection of the cage or aviary through flaming and the control of humidity. Periodical disinfection of the feeding and water bowls is required, and preventive administration of Dimetridazole in food is necessary. In this period it is good to administer some probiotic supplements (contain beneficial bacteria), which will help to rebuild the intestinal flora of the bird. Healthy greens and veggies will also help.

Eimeria (Coccidiosis)

It's a disease which is produced by parasites which are developing in the bird's intestinal tract. There are 9 species of Coccidia which belong to the genus Eimeria and can infect different parts of the intestine: Eimeria tenella, Eimeria acervulina, Eimeria mivati, Eimeria mitis, Eimeria necatrix, Eimeria maxima, Eimeria brunetti, Eimeria praecox, Eimeria again. It could affect youngsters between 10 days and three months old.

Treatment: administration of polivitamines, sulfonamides, vitamin K or antibiotics.

6. Maintaining hygiene prevents diseases.
Ascariasis

It's a parasitic disease caused by parasites (Ascaridia), which affects 3-4 months old young birds, turkeys, geese, pigeons, parrots, etc.... Ascaridia galli is a white-yellowish colored worm.

Youngsters can get infected orally through infested water or feed. Massive infestation with worms could lead to the blockage of the intestine, causing death if it's not treated.

Symptoms: weakness, anorexia, diarrhea, anemia, hypovitaminosis and the youngsters stop developing.

Treatments: piperazine salts are effective in treatments against ascariasis. Cambendazole in feed for 5 days. Fenbendazole (Panacur) in feed for 4 days. Mebendazol in feed for 7 days. Flubendazole in feed for 7 days. Disinfection of the cage or aviary through flaming and periodical disinfection of birds is required.

Toxoplasmosis

Toxoplasmosis is an infection caused by the parasite Toxoplasma gondii. Symptoms are fever, respiratory dysfunction, diarrhoea, paresis, paralysis, and convulsion.

Treatments: administration of sulfonamides; antibiotics; disinfection through flaming.

Disinfecting cats could prevent this.

7. The appetite and the digestive system
Diarrhoea

When a bird has diarrhoea, the droppings are very soft, even fluid, with a smell different from normal. The frequency of elimination of droppings will be very high.

Diarrhoea leads to dehydration of the bird and to loss of minerals of the organism. There are multiple causes:

- inadequate nutrition;
- bacterial infection of the intestines;
- intoxications;
- parasites.

The required treatment is focused on an antidiarrheal diet and specific medication for each situation.

You will need to feed your bird with some poppy seeds, because of their calming effect, boiled rice, some fried seeds and replace water with mint tea. You can add mashed boiled rice or some coal powder.

Antidiarrheal medication will be followed from your avian vet's advice. You can also offer your bird a special solution, which contains minerals, and it could be prepared at pharmacies:

NaCl (sodium chloride)	8.0 g
CaCl2 (calcium chloride)	0.13 g
KCl (potassium chloride)	0.2 g
MgCl (magnesium chloride)	0.1 g
NaH2PO4 (monosodium phosphate)	0.05 g
NaHCO3 (sodium bicarbonate)	10 g
Glucose	1.0 g

Distilled water	1000.0 ml

It`s very important to separate your bird from the others, to assure an adequate temperature of the room 77 - 95 degrees Fahrenheit (25 - 35 degrees Celsius) and a very strict hygiene routine.

Enteritis (Inflammation of the intestines)

Enteritis represents the inflammation of the intestines, and it`s one of the most frequent causes of mortality in cage and aviary birds.

The main causes of enteritis are:

- Nutrition;
- Bad quality food; inadequate composition of the food;
- Intoxication;
- Toxic plants, lead, etc....

Intestinal parasites

Tapeworms, eelworms, coccidia can harm the intestinal mucus.

Viruses

There are different kind of viruses; Paramyxoviruses and hepatitis viruses, which can also cause enteritis.

8. Bacterial infections

Salmonellosis and E. coli are pathogenic bacteria, which are the main causes of enteritis. The main symptom of enteritis is diarrhea. The feathers around the cloaca are dirty, the bird is lethargic, sad and sleeps too much. Because it has lost too much liquid, the affected bird will drink a lot of water. Laboratory investigations (bacteriological and parasitological analyses) will have to be done to discover the main cause of enteritis. Meanwhile, the bird has to be placed in a warm place, it will need infusions and forced feeding. Injection with vitamins will strengthen the immune system of the bird. The avian vet will prescribe the proper antibiotic treatment for your bird.

Some birds have a very big appetite, but they'll remain skinny because they suffer from parasitic infestation with acarians; Dermanyssus gallinae.

In this situation, you'll have to clean the cage or aviary, and internal and external disinfection is required. You need to offer them some hemp and poppy seeds, and iron sulphate in water.

If your bird refuses to eat and drink, then its life is in danger. The loss of appetite indicates an illness of internal organs, which could be very dangerous. In this case, you'll need to contact your avian vet as soon as possible.

Constipation

The signs of constipation are the enlarged abdomen of the bird and the missing fresh droppings on the cage floor. The impossibility of elimination of droppings leads to intoxication. In this situation, the cloacal orifice free opening is needed by administering a few drops of castor oil through the bird's beak, for two-three days. The bird will need a warm place, and for the next few days, the diet will contain honey, green plants, and fruits.

Obesity

Obesity could lead to health problems like heart and circulatory system disorders, joint problems or modification of the internal organs like liver fattening and constipation. The major problems are the impossibility of flying, loneliness, and overfeeding with flax and rape seeds.

The main measures that must be taken are the introduction of lettuce in the bird's diet and increase the frequency of free flight in the room.

You can replace the drinking water with dandelion tea, for 20 days (add 12-15 grams of dried dandelion leaves to 250 ml of hot boiled water). The obese bird will have to receive only half part of the usual daily seed portion. Green food and fruits can be offered daily.

Excessive weight loss

The excessive weight loss of the bird could have multiple causes like nutritional and parasitic problems. The suffering bird has dry skin and a very prominent breastbone.

When you observe these symptoms, you'll have to disinfect the cage and the bird and get dropping samples for further examinations. Your avian vet will inform you with a right diagnoses and will establish the treatment.

Capillaria (Capillary or Threadworms)

There are several species of Capillaria and can be found in the lower intestinal tract, causing severe inflammation of it. Disinfection of the cage and accessories is required with hot water and treatments with Hygromycin may be used.

Gastrointestinal parasites - Tapeworms

Tapeworms, which live in the bird's body, eliminate their eggs through the bird's feces. The eggs are consumed by intermediate hosts (earthworms, snails, and insects like grasshoppers, ants, beetles, flies, etc....). Inside of the intermediate hosts, a small embryo develops in the eggs but does not hatch immediately. When the bird is eating the infected insects or worms, the larvae in the egg reaches infection stage within two to three weeks, and they will become tapeworms in the bird's body. Wild parrots are infested with tapeworms when they eat insects and worms directly from the wild. Wild parrots, that were recently imported (captured from the wild) could have a prophylactic treatment against the tapeworm with Praziquantel.

Infestation with tapeworms is uncommon in domestically raised parrots.

Inflammation of the crop

The inflammation of the crop usually appears because of bacterial, fungal or parasitic infections. The dirty drinking water from the bowls can be the cause of the infection. If the water bowls are not cleaned at least once per day with hot water, then toxic mosses and dirt could form in the recipients. The affected bird is vomiting, and the feathers on the bird's head are dirty and sticky. The affected bird could also suffer from diarrhea and become very somnolent and lethargic. You'll have to increase the body temperature of the bird with a heating lamp. The avian vet will prescribe anti-inflammatory medication which has to be administered through the beak. Before the treatment with antibiotics, laboratory investigations should be completed for a precise diagnosis. In this period, the affected bird diet is based on soft food: boiled eggs, biscuit soaked in water, boiled rice, etc.... If the bird doesn't want to eat, you'll have to force feed it. Even if the bird has recovered, you'll have to take care of him/her a few weeks after. Otherwise, it will get sick again. You can warm up the bird when it's needed, and injection of vitamin A is required.

9. **Liver diseases**
Inflammation of the liver (Hepatitis)

The affected birds look tired, lethargic and have a lack of appetite. The affected liver is not able to help the body with detoxification. Most birds suffer from itching and feather plucking. Because of the inflammation of the liver, the bird's skin can show some inflammation, the urine color is white, and the feces are greenish-yellow. The main factors that trigger acute, chronic hepatic inflammations are bacterias, viruses, fungi, parasites or intoxications. The liver is increasing in size, but it's an organ with incredible regeneration power if the disease is discovered in time.

If the hepatic tissue is very affected, then it can't regenerate, and this is cirrhosis of the liver. The therapy for the cirrhosis is impossible. The evolution of it can be stopped when it is recognized in time. Treatments with liver protection medication could be done. The possible cause could be the perishable oily seeds. Hazelnut mold (Aspergillus flavus) which forms in wet weather on the nutshell, and it's extremely toxic for the liver. You'll have to check the quality of the nuts before you offer them to your bird, by tasting them. Try to use brands that are sold in stores and supermarkets, this way you'll have the chance to buy fresh nuts.

Fatty liver

It`s a disease which appears in overweight birds. The accumulation of fat excess in the liver cells makes the liver work improperly. The main symptoms are diarrhea and respiratory difficulties; the nails and the beak are overgrown. When the liver increases too much in size, the tissue of the liver could break up, and internal bleeding could appear, causing death. To avoid these kinds of situations, slow weight loss is needed, by reducing the consumption of oily seeds. Administration of vitamin E and liver protection medication and lots of exercises is recommended (outdoor flight) to regenerate the liver function.

10. Beak health problems

Deformed beak

When the owners don't offer cuttlefish bones to their birds, then their beak will overgrow, which will lead to the inability of the bird to feed and drink. If the beak is not cut back in appropriate time, the bird could die, due to the inability to feed itself. When the bird feeds mostly soft food instead of seeds, then it doesn`t use the upper and lower parts of its beak sufficiently. You'll have to replace the soft food with the right diet and offer some tree branches to your bird to chew. Some owners cut their parrot's beak even if it`s unnecessary, this way they will accelerate the growing process of the beak. The abnormal growth of the beak, in some cases, could be because of a serious health disorder.

Injuries of the beak

In birds that suffer from the malformed beak because of vitamins and calcium or phosphorus deficiency, the beak could break very easily, even when the bird tries to break the nutshells.

Administration of soft food, fruits and calcium is required, vitamin A application on the beak with a piece of cotton - wool, and a professional remediation of the broken beak made by an avian vet will give good results. Injuries of the beak could also happen because of accidents. There are several ways to reconstitute malformed or injured beaks. Prosthetic beaks are made by inserting pins into the bone of the existing beak, which is then covered by a dental acrylic material and shaped.

Soft beak

The beak of some birds becomes very flexible because of vitamin and calcium deficiency. In this case, the bird will need soft food, you'll have to grease the bird's beak with vitamin A and some calcium, and crushed eggshell administration is required. The main cause is vitamins A, C, biotin, pantothenic acid, folic acid, and calcium or phosphorus deficiency. Sometimes, on the beak, there could appear some exfoliation, which looks like scales. You must grease the beak with cod-liver oil or with vitamin A.

Respiratory system problems

Loud whistling sounds and hard breathing of the bird indicates a problem with its respiratory system. The birds are very sensitive to air currents, and they get cold very easily. To prevent these kinds of problems, you'll need to find a proper place for the cage.

When you hear these whistling noises, you must feed the bird with grated carrots and fruits and green plants rich in vitamin C.

The avian vet's help is needed to prescribe the right antibiotics for the bird.

Another respiratory problem is when the bird is breathing with the beak open. In this case, the bird`s tracheas are infested with a parasitic worm, called Syngamus trachealis.

Abundant nose secretions

The secretions in the nasal area indicate that the bird is sick. You can maintain the bird's body temperature by covering it with a piece of cotton cloth.

There are lots of secretions in the nose when the bird is suffering from mycotic, bacterial and viral infestations.

You have to avoid contact of your bird with other wild birds, and you must feed the bird with soft food, seeds soaked in milk, honey and chamomile tea. Vitamins A, C, and B complex intake are needed.

Acute respiratory insufficiency

Respiratory insufficiency is a symptom which usually appears in many and different kinds of health disorders. Respiratory difficulties can develop after the modification of the internal organs which are pressing the airways. When the thyroid gland increases in size, it can restrain the airways. All the internal organs are situated in the same cavity of the body (thoracic cavity and the stomach are not separated by a diaphragm as in mammals), and the modification of the internal organs may influence the respiratory functions negatively. The normal function of the air sacs and the lungs is affected by the increase of the liver, by obesity, sexual disorders and accumulation of excrements as a result of digestive diseases. When it`s a slow evolutionary process of the disease, the affected bird is flying less, not singing and sleeps too much. After all, the bird will lose its strength and yawns very often because of the lack of oxygen. The affected bird is breathing rapidly with an open beak. If the bird is not taken to the vet for consultation and treatment, the bird could suffocate.

Rhinitis

Rhinitis is an inflammation of the nostrils. The feathers around the nostrils are dirty, because of the abundant nose secretions. The nasal discharge can form a crust and can block the nasal orifices. The bird rubs his head on perches and on different objects of the cage to liberate his/her affected nostrils. The main cause of rhinitis is infection with viruses, bacterias or mycoplasmosis. Rhinitis is transmissible from parrot to human.

For this reason, the avian vet will administer an injection with antibiotics (Tetracycline). In case that the infection is resistant to Tetracycline, laboratory investigation is needed to find the proper antibiotic for the bird. Injections with Polyvitamins are also indicated and vitamin C (powder), (a pinch of vitamin C powder in 30 ml of water) added in drinking water to fight the infection. The nostrils and the feathers around it will have to be cleaned with cotton wool soaked in warm water a few times per day. The inflamed and red skin around the nostrils has to be greased with a special ointment, which contains fish fat, marigold (Calendula officinalis) and vitamin A. Because the body temperature of the bird drops, you'll have to warm it up, by placing a heat lamp or bulb (60-100W) near the cage. The "warming up " procedure has to be done until the bird has recovered.

You can also place a bowl filled with hot chamomile infusion in front of the cage. You'll have to cover the cage with a towel and try to direct the hot steams inside the cage. You can apply this method once or twice per day. Disinfection with hot water of the perches, feeding and drinking bowls is required. Rhinitis could affect those birds which live in preheated rooms, especially during winter. Because of the dry air, the bird's airways become affected. To control the humidity of the room, you can place a wet towel on the radiator. There is also special humidifying equipment, or you may also offer your bird the opportunity to have baths every day. You can also spray your bird daily with warm water.

11.Sense organs problems
The eyes

The bird's eye problems could have noninfectious and infectious causes. Noninfectious diseases are swollen eyelids (blepharitis), glaucoma, conjunctivitis, cataracts, and traumas.

Infectious eye diseases could appear in ornithosis, avian mycoplasmosis or chlamydiosis. Noninfectious eye problems could be treated with vitamin A (drops) applied to the eyes with cotton buds. You can also clean the eyes with chamomile tea.

The ears

There are rare cases of ear infections in birds. Usually, the bird is continuously scratching the infected ear, which means that the interior area is inflamed. The bird frequently shakes its head and holds its head on one side. You'll have to apply in one drop of boroglycerine in each ear. If the symptoms persist, then visit your avian vet for an antibiotic prescription.

12. Reproduction problems

Infertility of the cock

One of the main causes of the infertility of the cock is the unsuitable partner, and for this reason, the birds need to be watched during the mating period.

The stress, inadequate feeding, too young and too old age of the birds could be the reason for the infertility.

During mating period, the cock's diet should be increased with vitamin E intake.

The retention of the egg

A frequent problem in cage birds is the retention of the eggs. If the hen can't lay the egg, it could over press the internal organs. The impossibility to eliminate droppings can lead to self-intoxication. It can happen because of the age of the bird, the size and shape of the egg, the sudden drop of temperature from 53.6 degrees Fahrenheit (12 degrees Celsius) and the stress during the egg-laying process. At the first signs of the retention of the egg, wet heat will help in most of the cases. You'll have to place a bowl filled with hot water in front of the cage, which must be covered with a towel and the hot steam has to be directed towards the cage. A heating lamp or bulb (60 W) will be necessary near the cage and directed towards the suffering bird. You can also help your bird by introducing 0.5-1 ml of warm paraffin or comestible oil in the cloacal orifice with a plastic syringe (without a needle on top). This operation should continue each hour until the egg is delivered. In this case, for the bird's safe, vet intervention is required. The temperature in the room has to be maintained at around 86 degrees Fahrenheit (30 degrees Celsius).

13. Diseases of the feet
Abscess of the feet

The main causes of this disease are the circulatory disorders of the feet caused by insufficient movement, inappropriate perches and avitaminosis A (too little green food and fruits). First the abscess forms on the heel or under a toe (a pressure zone). The skin becomes very thin, the wound appears, and soon it will be covered with crust. The affected feet are swollen, and it`s very warm. The wound becomes an open injury, filled with pus. The crust has to be removed surgically, and the affected foot will be treated with medicated ointment. The affected bird will be supervised for 10 days. The bandage has to be changed in every 2-3 days. Injection with multivitamins stimulates the healing process. To spare the other foot, the perches must be wrapped with paper towel or with bandages, and they have to be fixed at the end of the perches with adhesive tape. All the perches available in the cage have to be wrapped because the bird will hesitate to sit on them.

If there are no pustules filled with pus on the bird's foot, it's enough to use an ointment with vitamin A or with fish fat or cod liver oil daily. During this treatment, the presence of the grit is not necessary for the cage, because it will stick on the bird`s foot and it will stop the healing process.

Offer your bird the opportunity to free-flight every day for 1-2 hours. This way the circulatory system and the blood circulation in the feet will be stimulated. The lack of movement and the overweight body of the bird has negative effects on the feet.

14. Accidents and injuries of the limb
Sprains and dislocations

Sprains appear after the wrong manipulation of the bird, or its leg is stuck between the bars.

The affected joints are inflamed causing pain, and the affected area is increasing in size. In the case of sprains, the treatment consists of the application of a bandage with wool balls soaked in alcohol and the settlement of the bird in a quiet place is required.

In the case of a dislocation, re-suspend the ends of the joints in the initial position and then maintain them in this position by applying adhesive tape around the hip joint.

You can feed your bird with poppy and hemp seeds, and everyday observation of the bird is required.

Fractures

Fractures appear as a result of accidents through manipulation or bumping of the bird.

The leg is dragged, and the opposite extremity of the fracture moves. The affected area is turgid, much bigger, infiltrated with blood and lymph. If the fracture is open, then the rupture of the muscle and skin can be observed, with the visibility of the bones.

The stages of the treatment are:

- the treatment has to be done maximum 48 hours after the accident;
- calming the pain with infiltration of painkiller;
- disinfection of the area with ethacridine lactate (Rivanol solution);
- removal of the impurities;
- immobilization of the area;
- attach a collar around the bird's head to prevent tearing the bandage;
- administration of antibiotics and vitamins, daily;
- supervision of the evolution of the fracture.

The advantage of surgical operation compared with traditional methods is that the fracture can be more perfectly remediated.

Gout

When uric acid levels become too high in the bird's bloodstream, then gout occurs. Birds don't usually produce much urine. The uric acid is removed from the blood by the kidneys and eliminated through the urine. When the kidneys don't work properly, the level of uric acid becomes too high in the bloodstream, and it will become crystallized. The feet are swollen and become a red-violet color. When the uric acid crystallizes in tissues, it will form small, white nodules. High doses of vitamin A and lots of fluids may be given, and stimulation of renal function by adding sucrose in drinking water could positively influence the evolution of the disease. Because of the swollen feet and painful nodules, the bird may be unable to perch, and so it will remain on the floor of the cage. The food and water bowls should be placed to easily accessible locations, by helping the bird to be able to eat and drink without any problem. The perches have to be wrapped with paper towels, and the cage has to contain little-wrapped platforms to help the bird to sit comfortably. Nodules could be eliminated surgically when they have a specific size. In this case, anesthesia is not recommended because it could harm the affected kidneys.

15. Nervous system problems

Twirling or Torticollis

They constantly throw their head back, walk around in a circle, turn their heads around in a circle and look up.

If there are cerebral diseases, then the bird needs to stay in a dark and quiet place on a piece of soft cloth.

There could be several causes:

- infections with viruses, bacteria, parasites, mycoplasma - administration of antibiotics is needed;
- intoxication with lead, insecticides - administration of antidote is required;
- injuries and brain hemorrhage;
- avitaminosis A and lack of calcium - administration of necessary substances;

-　　brain tumors.

Dizzy bird

The bird can't hold itself on the perch and could fall and hurt itself, causing serious injuries.

During flight, they can't appreciate the right distance. To avoid accidents, the floor of the cage must be covered with a thin piece of cloth. Free flight must be stopped until the clarification of the causes.

Intoxications of the cage birds

In intoxication with disinfection substances, the bird has difficulty in breathing and it has discolored eyes. The bird's life is in danger!

- Soap or deodorants: they contain a substance which could lead to temporary blindness. Washing the affected area with cold water is required.
- Alcohol: the bird is vomiting, it has fluffy feathers, stays in the corner of the cage, it's losing balance. Sick and old birds could die; healthy birds could recover by themselves.
- Toxic plants: digestive symptoms, diarrhea. You need to assure green plants in your bird's diet.
- Nicotine (cigarette buts): it can affect the nervous system, causing death. Don't leave cigarettes near the birds.
- Salt (and salty food): the bird is very thirsty, it is agitated and shaking. You'll need to administrate lots of water through the bird's beak. In severe situations, the bird could die.
- Teflon (from frying pans): suffocation and death in 30 minutes. Avoid keeping the bird in the kitchen; in case of accidents move the bird outside as fast as possible.
- Lead (newspapers, lead-based paint): green colored diarrhea (even the presence of blood), the kidneys, the bone's marrow and the nervous system are affected. If the accident is discovered in time, the administration of an antidote is required - calcium EDTA (amino polycarboxylic acid).

The major intoxications take place when the birds swallow the toxic substances. The owner could offer some milk with a dropper, and after that, the bird will start vomiting in a short time.

Another solution is the administration of medicinal coal. You'll have to dissolve 5 grams of medicinal coal in 50 ml of water. This preparation will need to be administered through the beak. Once you have carried out the operations described above, after one hour, you'll have to administer some oily purgatives, oil or castor oil.

Chapter 6: How to take care of your parrot

1. Beak and nails

The bird's beak and nails grow continuously, so you have to take care of them, throughout your bird's life.

To prevent the beak from growing excessively you need to place a cuttlefish bone in the cage, which is also high calcium intake, or you can cut the beak carefully with a strong pair of scissors. When the trimming process is taking place, for safer results (to avoid injuries), you need two people to do this. Parrots have a predisposition for excessive beak growth, so you'll have to cut it almost every four weeks. Because of the long beak, parrots can`t eat properly and they could die because of that. Before trimming the beak, dab it with slightly warm glycerin or olive oil.

When nails overgrow, you need to cut them very carefully with a special scissor without causing any injuries. Overgrown nails lead to instability on the perches or even the inability to walk.
When trimming the nails, it's best to cut off a little at a time. You have to know that the bird's nails contain (at the base of it) very fine blood vessels and nerves, which makes them very sensitive. If by mistake you cut too much from the bird's nails, they will bleed, and the bird will feel the same pain as we do when we overcut our nails. In this case, you can stop the bleeding by using cotton buds soaked in vitamin K or C.

For a better result, when you cut the nails, you can grease your bird's toes with comestible oil to soften them.

2. How to clip your parrot`s wings

If your parrot mostly lives in an aviary and you don't interact with it, then clipping the wing is unnecessary. The main purpose of wing clipping is to prevent rapid and upward flight.

Wing clipping is safe if it is performed properly. If you don't know how to clip your bird's wing, the best way is to find an avian vet who is experienced in the art of wing clipping. If you decide to do it by yourself, then you'll have to study the bird's wing shape and terminology of its feathers. You'll also need a competent assistant who will help to hold the bird. Avoid clipping the primary and secondary coverts, and secondary feathers on both wings. With the help of your assistant, wrap the bird in a towel and hold it by the neck.

Be careful, the bird's chest must not be restricted because it can't breathe and carefully liberate one wing which has to be held at the base of the humerus and not by the feathers. If you don't hold the wing correctly, you can cause serious injuries if the bird tries to flap its wing.

3. Bathing your parrot

In the wild, parrots can take a bath in rainy days by opening their wings and tail sideways or they can have a bath in little natural ponds on uneven ground.

In captivity, you have to provide different ways to keep your bird clean. You can spray them, or you can shower them, but you should be careful because the upper respiratory tract and the sinuses are quite exposed. You can provide them with artificial ponds by using water bowls, or you can also use the sink or the bathtub. However, your bird will still love to have a bath in its drinking water bowl.

Senegal parrots will let you know which way they prefer and enjoy their bath time. Always make sure that you use room-temperature water, do not use warm or hot water, because it will dry out their skin so they itch and can cause feather plucking/picking. The importance of giving a shower is to get them clean and encourage them to preen their feathers. In outside aviaries, some parrots enjoy a sprinkler system overhead or getting lightly sprayed with a water hose.

During bath and shower time parrots will typically fluff up their feathers to allow the water to penetrate through the feathers and to their skin. After bath time, your parrot will start preening and getting its feathers back in the position they normally were.

It is recommended that your bird is bathed during daytime and given time to dry completely. Some parrots would most likely prefer to get showered on a daily basis. For other birds, a good bath or shower once or twice a week will be enough.

During molting periods, your bird will become very itchy due to the new feathers coming out. You should increase bath time during this period, as it will help keep the itchiness down and also make the feather sheaths soft, making it easier for your parrot to remove them. Let your bird dry off naturally or with the help of a towel and make sure that your bird is placed in a warm room of the house. Then let your bird have the chance to preen and get its feathers back in place. The use of blow dryer can lower their skin moistness, and there is also the danger of possibly burning their skin.

Some parrots are scared to get wet, so if your bird doesn't like to bathe, then wait until it rains and lightly mist them with the spray bottle. Because they like to imitate us, just go ahead and get yourself wet or let them see you splash in the water. It is very important not to force your bird to bathe.

Sometimes your parrot will get dirty and greasy. In this kind of situation you'll have to use special shampoos. The best shampoos are those for children. There are also several special products for your bird, but be careful of those which contains oils and perfumes, because your bird could perceive them as detrimental substances and it may start to pull out his/her feathers. You'll have to dilute a little bit of shampoo in the bathing water and easily sprinkle your bird with it until it becomes all wet. Leave the bird for about five minutes in a warm place, then rinse it well with clean, warm water. If your bird is excessively dirty (oil, ink, liquid glue, etc.), then you'll have to visit your avian vet as soon as possible.

4. Flying exercises

Parrots belong to flying bird category, so they'll need to fly very often. So if you have a small cage in your house, you'll have to assure them with almost daily flying exercises, to maintain their well being. A room with well-closed windows will surely be enough for them. You have to avoid a small cage with lots of birds and toys. If you can't afford a bigger cage, then one pair of parrots should be enough for you. As long as they're with two, they will be alright.

Free flight will prevent muscle atrophy of the wings and chest, and it will maintain the bird in a good physical condition.

When you leave your bird outside of the cage, serious precautions have to be taken, because your bird could be everywhere, for example on the couch where it can be crushed when he is hiding between the pillows.

Another important problem is the kitchen for them, you should not leave the birds in the kitchen, especially when you are cooking because they can fall into a hot pan from the cooker. They love to sit on top of the doors, so you have to be careful when you close the door of your room.

Before the first flight you have to place your bird close to the window to get used to it, otherwise, it will try to fly through the window, and serious accidents could happen. You can also cover the window with some curtains to avoid accidents. In the wild, parrots "work" to provide their food, to build their nest, to fly and care for young ones. You'll have to make sure that your parrot will perform some exercises for five minutes, a few times every day.

Wing flapping: try to lower your hand up and down to encourage flapping. You can swing your parrot around in a circle or back and forth by making your bird flap its wings a few times a day. You can also place a blanket on the floor and chase your parrot around. They'll love this game.

You can also encourage your bird to dance with you and with your children. Your parrot will be very happy to dance and jump around and also will become tired. Make sure that children and parrots are supervised.

Bedding materials
In the wild, birds have less contact with their droppings, because they have unlimited space. In captivity, their droppings could affect the bird's health by the distribution of microbes and parasites.
Loose sand or absorbent paper are the best bedding materials; you should avoid using newspaper because it contains lead (chemical substance), which could be dangerous for your bird.
Parrots will need a daily portion of grit in their cage, to help with digestion, which will have to be changed daily because there will be droppings on them and this way you can maintain your bird's healthy life.

The everyday life of parrots
During the day, parrots will play by climbing on perches, singing or will wait for the owners to return home.

In the wild, parrots get up at sunrise and go to sleep at sunset.
In captivity, you have to respect the day and night program of the bird. So you have to be sure that your bird will spend most of the day in a room exposed to light and for that, you can place the cage close to the window.

At nighttime they will need a room without any illumination and noise source to have a good sleep. If you stay up for long and you have to use the light in the same room where the birds are, you better cover the cage with a thin piece of curtain material to help them sleep. You can use that piece of material also in daytime, to cover half of the cage, which will help the bird to take shelter from the direct sunlight when the weather is hot.

Inappropriate perches

In the wild, the birds sit on different sizes of branches, which are very comfortable for them. In captivity, they spend almost all the time on the perch, which could be too slippery, too thick or too thin for the bird's feet. All these imperfections can cause swelling of the feet and deformities of the joints.

To avoid these problems, you can place big branches in the cage, but first, you'll have to peel their bark, and for disinfection, you'll have to pour hot water on them. It's good to have different sized perches in the cage because it will stimulate the blood circulation and it will exercise the parrot`s feet. Sandy perches may dry out the feet and make them sore if they are the only perches provided in your parrot`s cage. These perches have fantastic value if they are positioned in the right place.

5. **How to prevent escape**

First of all, you have to clip your parrot`s wings to avoid high altitude flights and to assure an easy landing on the floor. You must always make sure that all the windows are well shut. Don't let out a bird if its wings are not clipped. When somebody is knocking at your door, before you open it, place the bird back in the cage. They could sometimes be scared when they see strangers, and they can fly outside through the door.

Make sure that your parrot can`t get out of the cage, some birds are extremely intelligent, and they're able to open the cage door with their beak, so you'll have to provide a lock for the cage door.
When your friends are visiting you at home, you better lock the cage for the bird`s sake, to avoid escaping through the open windows. In case your bird escapes, you have to have some recent pictures taken of your parrot.

If your bird just simply disappeared, then take the cage outside and put some fresh food and water in it, maybe your bird will try to return.

If your bird is on the nearest tree, then you can sprinkle some water on it with a garden hose. Be careful, the pressure of the water can cause serious injuries to your bird!

Be sure that you have all the necessary equipment at hand in case that the bird is reappears: towels, cage, nest, etc.

Contact your closest neighbors to give them a detailed description about your missing parrot and make sure that everybody knows your address and phone number to contact you in case they find your bird. Make posters with the bird's detailed description on and place them on light posts as far as possible around your area on main and side roads, shop stores, churches etc. Your children can help you by offering posters to their friends at school.

Ring local vets and give them your phone number and pet details. Walk around your local area calling your bird, don't forget that your bird is very scared and you'll have to call her very often because even if s/he hears you, s/he will not answer back to you for the first time. You'll have to return in the same places to call your bird again and again. Drop your poster into letterboxes in your area.
If you manage to find your bird, you'll have to visit your avian vet as soon as possible for a detailed examination and wing clipping.

Chapter 7: Trauma In Parrots

When the bird suffers a trauma without bleeding, then it has to calm down and stay warm. When the bird is bleeding, after breaking a leg or wing, first you have to stop the bleeding, then you have to calm the bird down. If the bird has suffered a cranial trauma, you don't have to place it in a warm place, because he will need a dark and quiet place. To stop the bleeding, you'll need to apply a cotton cloth on the wound, by pressing it for 5-10 minutes. The cotton cloth soaked in vitamin K is more efficient. Cuts and scratches must be cleaned with iodine.

If your bird is covered with a greasy substance, then you have to wash and dry it, or you can apply some talcum powder on it. In all the above situations try to find a vet as soon as possible.

1. Poor general condition

The normal body temperature of the birds is 105.8 degrees Fahrenheit (41 degrees Celsius). When they get sick, the body temperature drops too much, that's why you need to measure your bird's body temperature when you observe these kind of problems. You'll have to separate the sick bird from the others and keep it inside of the house.

All you have to do is to increase the bird's body temperature when it's too low by placing a desk lamp with a 75-100 W bulb at 10 cm close to the bird. The room has to be heated and the temperature has to be between 77- 95 degrees Fahrenheit (25 - 35 degrees Celsius).

2. Forced feeding

When the birds are sick, they usually refuse to eat; this could be a big problem because they can't survive for long without food.

It is, therefore, necessary to force your bird to eat, with viscous consistency mashed food, which is given little by little, with a syringe without needle on top. You can feed your bird 3-4 times per day with liquid food. If you don't know how to feed your bird, you better ask your avian vet to show you how to force feed your bird.

Because forced feeding is very stressful for birds, it has to be done just in case the bird hasn't eaten for 2-3 days. It`s important not to stress the bird!

3. Skin and feather problems

Massive molting represents the slow growth process of feathers. The affected birds have broken and disintegrated feathers.

There are multiple causes like food deficiency (the lack of amino acids, vitamins, and minerals), improper maintenance (insufficient light and humidity), liver or kidney disease or tumor or hormonal disorders.

Soft molting is a permanent or partial feather loss of the bird. The most important causes are a high level of humidity, with light and food deficiency.

French molting is characterized by the continuous growth and loss of feathers, without the possibility to cover all parts of the bird's body.

There are a few possible causes that produce french molting, like viruses (Polyoma or Circoviruses, which have the potential to inflame feather follicles), environment changes, hereditary problems, parasites and nutrition problems.

If you notice patches of bare skin on your bird's body or the molting process is not running normally, then you should visit your avian vet as soon as possible.

Xanthomas (Fatty tumors)

Xanthoma is a skin disease which affects overweight birds, especially parrots. Beneath the skin, there are deposits of fatty tumors, which have a yellowish color and can be found in the chest area, wing tips, and in ventral and femoral regions (between the legs and around the vent). Birds will cause self-trauma by pecking them. Xanthoma is a very common disease in birds which are fed exclusively on seeds. You'll need to introduce some millet, fruits, herbs and green leafy veggies in the bird's diet.

Once the bird gets all the necessary food, the existent fatty deposits will stop developing. Eczema should be disinfected with an antiseptic solution.

Chapter 8: Teaching Your Parrot

1. Before You Train

Even before you begin to train your bird, you need to learn your bird's body language. After all, he's an expert at reading yours! Body language is your bird's primary line of communications with you.

To effectively train your parrot, you need to be able to tell when he's frightened or distressed by your actions. A parrot who exhibits either of these emotions just isn't capable of learning. If he's busy worrying about your next move, he'll be preoccupied with defending himself.

If you discover that your parrot is in this emotional state when you're training him, you can give him a treat to see if he settles down. If not, then halt the session. Whatever you do, don't force your parrot to do something that he's not willing to do.

2. Reading Your Parrot's Body Language

Look into your parrot's eyes. Beautiful, aren't they? Look a little more closely and you'll notice that, unlike you and me, your parrot can control the size of his iris. This is the portion of the eye that gives him his eye color. He'll change the size of his iris if he's angry, frightened or feeling aggressive. This is called "flashing" or "pinning."

Understanding this gives you an indication of your friend's mood. Take time to note this action and place it into the context of the activity you and he are participating in. If eye pinning or flashing occurs while you're training, you may want to end the session or try to ease his fear or anger.

Is your bird doing an impersonation of a bat by hanging upside down? Don't be alarmed! Some species of parrot hang upside down. Read it as a sign that he's happy and content with his home.

Your parrot thinks he's a chicken? If you see him busily scratching at the bottom of the cage, it's normal behavior. Many parrots forage on the ground for food, and foraging is actually a socialization mechanism.

The posture of your parrot can speak volumes about how he's feeling. If your bird is relaxed, then you'll notice that s/he holds the head at attention. This indicates s/he's happy and content. If your parrot holds this position rigidly, it may be trying to show you just where its territory is.

A few behaviours

Your parrot is a natural-born vocalizer, but the type of sounds your bird makes can go a long way to telling you exactly what he's feeling.

Singing, whistling, and talking. These sounds are signs of a healthy and content parrot. You may have a bird who is a natural entertainer and this is his way of putting on a show.

Your bird may also chatter – you'll know the sound when you hear it. Whether it's loud or soft, it can signal one of two things: Either your friend is content or he's beginning to learn to talk. If he's chattering rather loudly, though, consider the fact that he's attempting to get your attention. If you notice that he chatters in the evening before going to sleep, he's trying to connect with other flock members.

And you thought only cats purred. The purr of a parrot is similar to a growl, but like a cat's purr, it is a sign of contentment. Sometimes, though, a purr may actually be a signal that he's annoyed with something. To read this vocalization properly, look at the context of the entire environment he's in at the moment.

Further, your parrot, at times, may click his tongue against his beak. Don't be concerned about this. Usually this is just to entertain himself. He may also be asking you to pet him or to pick him up.

Growling is a form of aggressive vocalization and not all birds do this. If yours does, take a look at its surroundings. Remove anything that you think may be bothering it. A word of caution, don't try to pick up or touch your parrot when it growls.

Wings

In addition to flight, parrots use their wings for communication. Your friend may display his emotions in three distinct ways; flapping, flipping or drooping.

If your parrot is flapping his wings or flying in one place, he's actually exercising, trying to get your attention, or just being happy. Birds may also use their wings simply to stretch or as a built-in fan – to cool themselves.

Your friend may perform wing flipping for several different reasons. Perhaps he's angry or in pain. He may also just be fluffing his feathers in order to get them to lay properly. If he's performing this activity while hunching over and bobbing his head (I'm sure you've seen this in some birds), it means he's hungry.

The drooping of wings normally indicates that your friend isn't feeling well. This is especially true if your bird is a little older. If, however, your friend has recently taken a bath, she may droop her wings to allow them to dry. Youngsters' wings may also droop as they attempt to master the skill of folding and tucking in their wings.

3. Reading Your Parrot's Feathers

One may not have thought of this, but a parrot performs body language even with her feathers. If your bird has ruffled his feathers, he may have done this during the preening process. This action helps to remove dirt and feather dust. In addition, it helps to return the feathers to their proper position.

Your bird may also ruffle his feathers to relieve pent-up tension or even to keep warm. Don't overlook the fact that ruffled or fluffed feathers could also mean a sign of illness.

The Crest Position

Parrots have large expressive crests. When relaxed, the crest is held back with just the tip tilted upwards; when excited, birds may lift their crest.

If the crest is lifted extremely high, this could be an indication of either fear or excitement. Approach your bird carefully until you can decide his emotion.

If the crest is flat, then your bird is either alarmed or feeling aggressive. This is especially true if he displays this while crouching and hissing.

If your bird quivers his feathers, this could indicate that he's frightened or excited. The quivering is also a natural part of his breeding behavior.

Oh, yes, your parrot uses his tail just as your dog or cat does. Movements in this body part can yield some clues about how he's feeling.

Look at Polly. Isn't it cute when she wags her tail? When your parrot wags his tail, like a dog, he's telling you he's happy to see you. As with all parrot body language, tail wagging can have several meanings; one being that he's preparing to defecate.

Fanning of the tail feathers is a clear sign of aggression or anger on the part of your bird, while tail flipping is another sign of overall happiness. Your bird flips his tail when he's glad to see you, plays with his favorite toy or gets a treat.

4. **Tail Movement Signaling Respiratory Distress**

How can you tell if your bird has exercised and is trying to catch his breath? Instead of looking for heavy breathing as we do when we overdo it, look to the tail. If his tail is bobbing, then he may be trying to recover from some strenuous exercise. A bobbing tail may also indicate respiratory distress. Take her to a veterinarian if you suspect this.

Bird Legs

Even a bird's legs and feet give you some indication of her emotions and state of health. When your parrot taps his feet, he's not trying out for some Broadway musical; he's actually gaining dominance over his perceived territory. He feels that someone or something is threatening it.

Some parrots develop what's called "weak legs." They simply don't want to stand or perch. Though this may look worrisome, don't be too concerned. This occurs most often after you've handled your friend. This is only his way of resting. Don't ignore it either; hold him a little longer and once he's felt he's been given his due amount of attention, he'll become strong enough to perch again.

The beak and head

Your parrot uses his beak for several tasks: grooming, cracking open nuts and seeds, building a nest, self-defense etc. The beak can also tell you various things about your parrot, if you're willing to read the signs and know what to look for.

If your parrot is grinding his beak, it's usually a sign of contentment. You'll hear this sound normally as he's dozing off to sleep at night. You'll know it the moment you hear it because it sounds like the beak is sliding from one side to another or one portion of the beak over another.

Click. Click. Click. Do you hear that? If your friend clicks his beak, it can indicate several things. First, if she does this only once, then pins her eyes (enlarges her iris), she is merely greeting you or acknowledging something.

If she performs several clicks in a row this is a clear warning that something is wrong. Under no circumstances should you handle her at this point. Beak clicking is most often confined to the cockatoo and cockatiel species.

When your parrot wipes her beak on a perch, the floor or sides of the cage or elsewhere, it could mean that she has incredibly good table manners or that she's marking her territory.

When thinking about parrots' beaks, biting somehow comes to mind. If your bird bites, there is always a reason. If you carefully examine your parrot's environment, you're bound to discover the reason. It could be that your friend feels that her territory is threatened for whatever reason.

Being aware of "pre-bite" movements will help you avoid being the object of the bite. A bird preparing to bite crouches and hisses before he takes any action.

If your parrot seems to be chewing everything, he's probably just entertaining himself. Providing several safe toys will keep him from chewing on any of your stuff!

5. Regurgitation: The Ultimate Parrot Compliment
If this has ever happened to you, you may have been a little taken aback – perhaps even horrified. Regurgitating (expelling food from his mouth, esophagus, and crop) is a parrot's way of showing affection. You'll know it's coming because your friend pins her eyes, bobs her head and stretches her neck before she regurgitates.

This is the same method she would use to feed her children. It's also an action that mating pairs perform for each other. Whatever you do, please, don't act horrified; you should praise your parrot for this.

Has your bird tried to grab your mouth yet? Hopefully she has. Although it may sound strange, "mouthing" is actually a method of parrot play. They grab each other's beaks and wrestle and joust with them.

6. Bowling for Parrots
"Bowling" is when a parrot crouches, holds her head tipped down toward you and bobs her head. She's actually asking to be petted or scratched.

If she assumes this position with a relaxed pose and raised wing – minus the head bobbing – she wants attention from you or a potential mate.

If she crouches with her head down, her eyes pinned and flaring tail feathers, you need to read this body language differently. This is especially true if her tail feathers are flared, her feathers are ruffled and her body is rigidly held while at the same time, she's weaving from side to side. All this combined is a definite sign of aggression.

Accentuate the Positive

Positive reinforcement is, without a doubt, the most effective method of training your bird. Don't limit your use of positive reinforcement to the times when your parrot seems distressed. This form of training is actually incredibly effective.

Besides that, the concept is deceptively simple. When your parrot performs an activity you want to encourage, you simply reward him with some type of treat. At the same time you're rewarding him with a treat, praise him. He'll get the picture much quicker than you can imagine.

When your parrot behaves in a way you would rather discourage, don't yell, scream or even punish him (trust me, none of those three would do absolutely no good), instead, ignore the behavior.

Your parrot wants nothing more than your attention. If his actions produce your attention, he really doesn't care if his behavior is bad or good.

Eventually, you'll be able to praise him without the need for a "treat" every time.

7. No Marathon Training Sessions

Sure, your parrot is smart, but his attention span is short. If you decide to conduct a marathon training session, it'll prove counterproductive. The most effective – and quickest – way to train a parrot is with short sessions. Schedule them frequently and make them a regular habit.

8. Repetition: The Key to Good Training

While repetition is indeed the key to good training, it needs to go hand in hand with another habit: consistency. This is especially true when you're training your parrot to talk. Let's say for example that you want to teach your parrot to say "mmm, food." Repeat the phrase frequently and consistently. Every time you feed him, say the phrase. Your parrot will soon associate these words with receiving food. The next thing you know, he will repeat them when he's hungry.

Be enthusiastic when you say these words to your parrot. Say them a little louder than your normal conversational tone. When you teach him other words, also repeat them throughout the day to him.

Just as you watch your language around young children, you really do need to watch what you say around your parrot. While you think you may be teaching your parrot, "Polly wants a cracker," he may also be learning other, less desirable, words from you or other family members.

Where to Start

If you're not quite sure exactly how to start your parrot's training program, consider the game "peek-a-boo." It's not only good training for your new friend; it's effective training for you as well. Never played peek a boo with a parrot? You're in for a real treat!

This is a great starter activity in which both you and your friend can create a safe environment for your interaction. You'll need a bath towel for this training session.

Your parrot will especially appreciate this because he is a "cavity nester." This means that he spends a great deal of time surrounded by objects – in the wild this would be tree branches – peeking out from under them. Carefully lay the towel over your parrot. Be patient, because he'll eventually peek out; when he does, say "peek a boo!"

Don't be afraid to alternate who gets covered by the towel. Place the towel over your head. When you look out from it, say "peek a boo!"

Both you and your friend will enjoy this game immensely. This is also a wonderful bonding exercise! This game most certainly can set the mood and the foundation for some very productive training.

9. **Window Training**

Keeping your new friend from flying into windows is important for his safety. Without a doubt, this would have disastrous consequences for him. Train him to be window-safe by taking your parrot to every window in the house and touching his beak to the glass. Do this several times a day for a few days so that your parrot understands he can't fly through the glass.

10. **Screaming**

You may have already discovered that screaming and squawking can be rather irritating. The good news is screaming doesn't have to be part of owning a parrot. You can train your bird not to scream – or at least keep the noise to a minimum. Do realize, however, that your parrot is a "born talker." Given the type of tongue he has and the highly developed larynx, it's inevitable that he'll make some type of noise. He loves nothing better than to "vocalize" his feelings, and his talking or squawking is his means of communication, whether warning his brethren of danger or celebrating the rising and setting of the sun everyday.

Vocalization and "singing" are just part of his normal behavior. Incessant squawking or screaming are not signs of normal behavior. A parrot usually screams excessively because of perceived stress. Your job – and granted, this is the more difficult aspect – is to find what's causing your parrot's stress.

It could be just about anything from a nutritional deficiency to the loss or addition of a family member, loneliness, boredom, fear, lack of sleep and even jealousy. Think of anything that may cause you undue stress and it can probably affect your parrot as well.

Your first stopgap measure, of course, is to stop or at least minimize the screaming. Start with attending to his immediate environment. Ensure that at a minimum all of his needs are met. Then you can at the very least eliminate this as a possible cause.

Next, you'll want to give him plenty of attention and a little more time with you. Ensure that he has enough toys to play with so you can cross off the "boredom" cause.

Keep a log of his screaming episodes while you're evaluating the situation to see if you can find some common denominator that connects all of them. If you can detect a pattern, you can begin to tackle the problem.

Is My Parrot Lonely or Tired?

If you've decided your parrot is lonely, the solution is to spend more time with him. In fact, for the first few days you've discovered this, don't leave his side. Allay his loneliness this way.

Is your bird tired? Perhaps moving it to quieter quarters at dusk will help him get a more restful sleep. Keep in mind that your parrot requires 12 hours of sleep at night. He sleeps from sunset to sunrise. He can't be up with the family every night watching television.

11. Teaching Your Parrot To Talk

Again, consistency and repetition (and patience!) are the keys to success. Remember that not all parrots develop the ability to speak, but rest assured with practice, the two of you will develop a special "language" of your own.

Don't expect your friend to talk in words that contain many syllables –at least not at first. Keep your training to one or two syllable words.

Designate one person in your household to teach him words. If everyone is talking at him, he'll get confused. He won't understand that you're trying to get him to repeat the lessons.

Concentrate on one word at a time rather than inundating him with several. If you want to teach him the word "food" that's great. Wait until he learns this one before you move on to another.

You'll want to repeat the word over and over for him. Every time you see him, say this word. Some parrot parents even tape the specific word so it may be repeated the maximum number of times. The parrot then can hear it throughout the day.

The more you talk to your parrot, the more he'll be interested in responding. Talk to your bird throughout the day just like he were a little person. Say "Good morning" when you wake up and "Good night" in the evening. Enthusiasm is also important when you're speaking.

When you go off to work in the morning, tell him you're going to work. Tell him you'll be back soon. Greet him when you get home. One Yellow-Naped Amazon parrot says "Hi Genius" (her name) whenever anyone comes in!

Don't be shy or feel foolish about talking with your parrot. Doing this is teaching him how to communicate and is the ultimate link between the two of you. It also teaches him familiar words.

Parrots are very smart animals. In addition to the specific words you're teaching him, he just may learn some others (hopefully good words!) along the way.

Chapter 9: How To Hand Feed A Baby Parrot

The maximum quantity which has to be given to a baby parrot before the weaning period has to be 10% of its body weight. The crop of most baby parrots usually gets emptied between 4-6 hours. You'll have to stop feeding the bird during night time, between midnight and 6 o'clock, (pause of 6 hours), a period which will allow the crop to empty of residual food. In this time you'll have enough time to get some rest. As the baby parrot grows, you'll have to reduce the number of feeding times, but you'll have to increase the quantity of food a little bit more. The most important thing is to control the quantity of food offered at each meal. Don`t offer more food than 10% of the bird's body weight in a meal. As the baby parrot grows, it will refuse to be hand fed, and you'll have to stop with hand feeding, or you'll have to reduce it. When you are at the stage of only 2-3 hand feedings, offer your bird solid food (softened pellets) or cooked food. In 2-3 weeks time, your bird should get used to solid food, and you can completely skip the evening meals.

How to prepare the hand feeding formula:

Use commercially prepared hand feeding formula which is specifically created for Senegal parrot babies.

You should use a thermometer to ensure that the hand feeding formula is warm enough (about 102 to 105 degrees Fahrenheit).

Use the microwave to heat up the water, add a measured amount of formula and stir. Make sure you feed at the right temperature.

Baby parrots develop much better on a thin formula rather than a thick one.

There are two most common methods of feeding; by syringe or spoon. Allow the bird to breathe between bites of food and stop feeding when the crop is nicely rounded. You can feed this formula up to 8 weeks of age. At this time you can start introducing weaning food in the bird's diet. Start weaning your baby with veggies, seeds, fruits and good quality pellets. Grains and sprouted seeds are also a good start in weaning your baby parrot because the softened shell is easier to break. Place a separate water dish next to his food. Any remains must be removed after 3 hours. At 13 weeks of age, your baby parrot should be placed on a single feeding per day. At this time pellets and seed mix should be its favorite food. Serve fruits and veggies cut into small pieces.

You can serve warm moistened pellets early in the morning at 8 am and 4 pm.

At the age of 16 weeks, your bird should be eating on its own.

During the weaning period, some babies can lose up to 15% of their weight.

It is important to keep an eye on your young bird regularly, regarding feeding. Watch your young bird's weight until it is five months old. Take your bird in your hand at least once a day and feel its breastbone by moving your hand from side to side across his/her chest. A healthy young parrot should have its breastbone covered with soft muscles on each side of it.

When you want to bring home a young Senegal parrot, make sure the feed pots are placed on the bottom of the cage. The climbing skill is not yet developed, and so the easiest way to feed themselves will be from the pots placed on the bottom of the cage.

Other foods can also be offered to your baby, like a chopped hard boiled egg, scrambled egg, chopped roast chicken breast, white boneless fish, a few sprinkles of grated cheese, boiled rice or pasta, biscuit crumbs, millet spray, boiled sweet potato mash, etc.

Here is a delicious recipe for young parrots:

1 and 1/2 cups fresh corn

1 cup brown rice

1/2 cup dried mango or banana

2 and 1/2 tbsp. raisins

3 and 1/2 tbsp. split lentils or peas

2 and 1/2 tbsp. unsalted pistachio nuts

one tsp. dried powdered milk

Bring 0.5 liters of water to boil, add all contents, cover and boil gently for 30 minutes. Serve warm or cool.

1. **Adding medication to drinking water**

Adding medication to drinking water is a controversial method, but sometimes this is the only available method. The purpose is for the bird to take medicine during the day directly from the drinking water. There are lots of disadvantages of this method. The bitter taste of the water makes the bird refuse to drink it. Some birds will refuse to drink water if its color has changed. Another disadvantage is that the water-medicine mixture has to be prepared and changed daily. There is a risk that your bird could dehydrate.

2. **Adding medication to food**

This method is better than the one with water because you can hide the medicine in the favorite food of your parrot. Usually, you can mix suspensions (liquid medicines), tablets or the content of a capsule of food.

The disadvantage of this method is that the bird could refuse to eat the food mixed with medicine because it changed the food taste. It could be difficult to mix the medicine with the food, because of the hard consistency of the medicine, and could be needed to add some water to soften the medicine.

The other disadvantage is, if there are several birds in the cage, all the others may eat from the medicine-food mixture. If a healthy bird is more authoritative, it could eat most of the food- medicine mixture, while the sick bird will receive too little.

Liquid medication (Suspensions)

This is the best method to administer liquid medication to your bird directly through the beak. Most oral suspensions are accepted very well by the birds, especially those with good taste.

You'll have to follow this procedure:

Fill the syringe or pipette with the prescribed quantity of suspension. There should be no needle on the syringe. Before you try restraining your bird, it's worth seeing if s/he will accept the suspension from the syringe through the cage bars. If not, you'll have to take out your parrot from its cage and wrap it in a towel, only the head and the chest of the bird will be uncovered and the chest also needs to be able to rise and fall for your bird to breathe. Before you start to administer the suspension, you'll have to wait until the bird calms down. You'll have to place the syringe at the left or right side of the beak, (it's possible that bird will bite it at first) and after you managed to place it in the interior of the beak, you can administer the suspension very slowly. You'll have to allow the bird to swallow frequently because if you squeeze the suspension too fast, the medicine can get into the lungs and the bird could die.

It's possible to observe that the suspension is coming out through the nostrils of the bird. Don't panic, just stop giving any medicine to your bird and leave it to calm down. Try to call your avian vet and tell him about what happened. If you can't reach your avian vet, then don't administer any medicine to your bird at that moment, until you speak with a specialized avian vet.

Injectable medications

Another method of administering medication is through repeated injections. Usually, this kind of method is not used very often, (only in emergency cases) because the bird is exposed to repeated stress because of the pain.

3. **Vitamins and minerals excess or deficiency**
The insufficient, or too much quantity, of vitamin intake can cause serious health problems to the birds. The owners have to assure them an optimal intake of vitamins and minerals.

Vitamin A

Vitamin A deficiency is considered the main cause of diseases in cage birds. In the bird's body, carotene is transformed into vitamin A.

Sources: provitamin A, fish fat or cod liver oil, egg yolk, carrots, green plants, vegetables, sunflower seeds.

Diseases: avitaminosis A: drying of the surface of the eyeball, eyelid edema, infections of the mucous membranes, rhinitis, sinusitis, white membranes inside the beak, kidney problems and gout (gout occurs in birds when uric acid level becomes too high in their bloodstream), swollen feet, diarrhoea, fluffed plumage; in molting period the slow growth process of feathers.

Properties: protects the mucous membranes, the eyes, and skin.

Administration: fish fat or cod liver oil 3-4 drops through the beak;

Vitamin B complex:

Sources: cereal germs, rice bran, raw egg yolk, carrots, oranges, other fruits, fresh cottage cheese, cooked liver, beer yeast.

The beer yeast must be dissolved in warm water before the administration. The preventive doses must be administered daily, until the bird will be perfectly healthy: 5-10 years old bird must have 50 mg beer yeast/day, 11-20 years old bird must have 100-150 mg beer yeast /day, 21-30 years old bird must have 200-250 mg beer yeast/day, 31-40 years old bird must have 300-350 mg beer yeast/day, 41-50 years old bird must have 400-450 mg beer yeast/day, 51-60 years old bird must have 500-550 mg beer yeast/day, 60-70 years old bird must have 550-600 mg beer yeast/day, 70 years old bird must have 650-800 mg beer yeast/day.

Diseases: the bird can`t keep its head straight;

-        avitaminosis B1: slowing growth rate, body weight loss, nerve problems, paralysis, spasms, digestive disorders, diarrhea.

Properties: it's given during hatching period, in growth period, in prolonged treatments with antibiotics to protect the intestinal flora.

- B5- in circulatory disorders;

- B12- in period of growth, agitation and depression;

Administration of B5 and B12 is given in liquid form, a couple of drops through the beak or in drinking water. You must add 1-2 ml of B complex in 50-100 ml of water for 3-5 days.

Vitamin C

Sources: green plants, bananas, grapes, blackcurrant, rose hips, parsley.

Diseases: the fragility of very small blood vessels, hematomas, tiredness.

Properties: increases immunity, strengthens the capillary wall.

Administration: feeding with green plants.

Vitamin D

Sources: green plants, egg yolk, fish flour, beer yeast, exposure of the bird to natural sunlight.

Diseases: slowing growth, fluffed plumage, rachitis, bone fragility, calcium deposits, lack or softening of the eggshell.

Administration: fish fat or cod liver oil - first a few drops through the beak, then mixed with food.

Vitamin

Sources: hemp seeds, dill, fruits, spinach.

Diseases: slow clotting, prolonged bleedings in subcutaneous tissue.

Properties: it's important in blood clotting.

Vitamin E

Sources: maize, cereal germs, yolk, butter, vegetables.

Diseases: decrease of fecundity, atrophy of embryo in egg, loss of coordination of muscles, walking in circles.

4. First aid kit for your parrot

It`s very important to have a first aid kit in your house because sadly, accidents can happen sometimes. First, you'll have to call your avian vet, but you have to be ready to use your first aid kit in case your bird requires immediate medical care in cases like burn or injury of one of the wings.

The first aid kit has to contain the following items:

- electric bird pillow, to warm up the bird to treat shock. In case your bird is very sick, don't leave it unattended on the pillow because there is a danger of overheating;
- Pedialyte (electrolyte solution for children), this kind of solution has to be given at room temperature;
- eye drops (medication) and eyewash (to clean the eyes);
- eyedropper;
- cotton swabs and balls to clean the open wound;
- scissors;
- gauze rolls to bandage scratches, burns or open wounds;
- tweezers to remove broken blood feathers;
- antiseptic wipes;
- betadine or iodine solution;
- medical tape;
- masking tape;
- 3% hydrogen peroxide solution to clean wounds. When you clean the wound for the first time, you'll have to use the undiluted form of the solution. After that, you'll have to dilute the hydrogen peroxide solution with water 1:10;

- medical first aid pen flashlight, to see inside of the bird's mouth;
- antibiotic ointment to prevent infection of cuts and scratches;
- syringe (without a needle on top), feeding tubes, pipettes. You have to be well prepared before you use feeding tubes;
- towels;
- hand feeding formula (mature birds can get 5% of their body weight at one feeding, once or twice per day);
- latex gloves;
- animal poison control center phone number;
- magnifying glass;
- heating lamp;
- bird`s medical records;
- parrot`s first aid book.

Conclusion

If this book has only been able to provide you with a brief view of the joys of parrot parenthood, then it's done its job. As you can plainly see, raising a parrot is more like raising a child than owning a pet.

If you choose a parrot as a baby, you and he experience a bond that is not unlike that of a mother and child. You'll not only be the proud owner of a beautiful parrot, but you'll experience a bonding on a far greater level than with an "ordinary" pet.

You two will eventually learn how to communicate – even if your friend doesn't learn how to speak entirely. He'll read your body language; you'll read his. Before you know it, you'll become nearly inseparable.

Adopting and raising a parrot is a lifelong commitment to love and care for a new friend, which will bring you many years of joy and fun.

Once you choose one of the many varieties of parrots available to you, you'll find that the other key elements of raising a parrot – from preparing your household to bring him home, to feeding him a proper diet and even training him – all fall into place. Why? Because every one of these actions, you'll learn, is performed from love.

Remember, though, that raising your parrot takes time, effort and dedication. The element that most surprises new parrot owners are the range of human-like emotions of parrots. Perhaps this is why the bond between parrot and human is so strong.

Parrot ownership is an exciting world. You may decide to raise one parrot or provide him with a friend, or even breed these astonishing birds. Whatever your decision, you're off to a great start.